GREAT RUGBY HEROES

A HISTORY OF RUGBY LEGENDS OF YESTERYEAR

GREAT RUGBY HEROES

A HISTORY OF RUGBY LEGENDS OF YESTERYEAR

Geoff Tibballs

MICHAEL O'MARA BOOKS

First published in Great Britain in 2003 by
Michael O'Mara Books Limited
9 Lion Yard, Tremadoc Road
London SW4 7NQ

A CIP catalogue record for this book is available from the British Library

ISBN 1-84317-046-9

1 3 5 7 9 10 8 6 4 2

Designed and typeset by Design 23

www.mombooks.com

Printed and bound in Singapore by Tien Wah Press

CONTENTS

INTRODUCTION

Rather like an Oscar acceptance speech where actors thank everyone from the director to the tea lady, I feel I should begin by mentioning some of those who, for one reason or another, just failed to make it into the final list of *Great Rugby Heroes*.

In a perfect world there would have been room for the likes of South African scrum-half Joost van der Westhuizen, the Scotland lock Gordon Brown (immortalised as 'Broon Frae Troon'), All Blacks Michael Jones and John Kirwan, Ireland full-back Tom Kiernan, Welsh centre Bleddyn Williams, Scottish flanker John Jeffrey ('The Great White Shark'),

'Broon FraeTroon' won 30 caps for Scotland at lock between 1969 and 1976

England's 100-cap man Jason Leonard, former France No. 8 Walter Spanghero, and Australian centre and dual World Cup winner, Tim Horan. If it's of any consolation, guys, it was tough leaving you out. With the exception of Argentina fly-half Hugo Porta whose talent

Full-back Tom Kiernan scored all of the 1968 British Lions test points in South Africa bar one try

Jason Leonard's first of over 100 appearances for England was against Argentina in 1990

would surely have merited a place in any national team, the final fifty names featured here come from the principal eight rugby-playing countries – namely England, Scotland, Ireland, Wales, France, South Africa, Australia and New Zealand. Players from emerging rugby nations such as Italy, Romania and Fiji may well warrant inclusion in any future edition but until they have consistently acquitted themselves at the highest level, priority must be given to the established teams. In making the selection, I was keen to give fair representation to each of the big eight, thereby resisting the temptation to concentrate on stars from the southern hemisphere at the expense of Six Nations players. After all, it would not be the most exacting task in the world to name fifty rugby heroes from New Zealand alone. Every nation has its heroes, and goal machine Ollie Campbell was just as much a folk hero to the Irish in the 1970s as was Grant Fox to the All Blacks a decade later.

The other trap I have endeavoured to avoid is that laid by statistics. The record books tell us that modern players are far superior to their predecessors – they win more caps and therefore score more tries, kick more penalties and so on. But this is largely because there is far more rugby played these days than even 25 years ago. To judge players' relative merits solely on statistics would be a dangerous, foolhardy approach – one that would eliminate almost everyone who wore a rugby shirt before 1970. For example, the Welsh points-scoring lists are dominated by Neil Jenkins. A fine player certainly, but how many Welshmen think he is a better fly-half than 'The King', Barry John?

It is, of course, impossible to make definitive comparisons between players of different eras. We can have no idea how the likes of Wavell Wakefield, Jackie Kyle or Hennie Muller would have fared in the modern game, but their contributions to the development and enjoyment of rugby football were immense. Some say Gareth Edwards would struggle in today's game – but that's only because he's 56 now!

As well as covering the different countries and eras, I have tried to include a cross-section of styles. Just as the top scorer in soccer inevitably attracts more attention than the midfield ball-winner, it is important to recognise the work done by the unsung heroes in the pack and not to be seduced solely by the dazzling footwork and lightning acceleration of the backs. Thus the book includes players from all positions. There are brilliant full-backs such as J.P.R. Williams, Serge Blanco and Gavin Hastings; exciting wingers like David Campese, Rory Underwood and Jonah Lomu; fleet-footed centres in Jeremy Guscott, Philippe Sella and Danie Gerber; majestic fly-halves including Barry John, Mark Ella and Rob Andrew; dynamic scrum-halves such as Gareth Edwards, Nick Farr-Jones and Dickie Jeeps; and powerhouse forwards like Colin Meads, Willie John McBride and John Eales.

If your favourite player is not included in the following pages, I apologise. But, trust me, it is no easy job sifting just 50 men from a game that has produced hundreds of world-class performers.

Geoff Tibballs

ROB ANDREW

It took a long time for Rob Andrew to be accepted as England's first choice fly-half. He was perceived as being too reliant on the boot, persuading critics to champion the cause of Bath's Stuart Barnes who was known to favour the running game. The rivalry between the two men occasionally threatened to go beyond the bounds of healthy competition, not least because Barnes made no secret of the fact that he considered himself to be the better player. Even in the face of West Country hostility, the selectors stayed loyal to Andrew, restricting Barnes to the odd crumb from the table. Their faith had already been repaid many times over by the time of the 1995 World Cup in South Africa. With the outcome of the quarter-final against Australia on a knife-edge going into the last minute, Andrew launched a beautifully composed dropped goal to snatch victory for England 25-22. At 32, Rob Andrew had finally come of age. Almost overnight those who had been his greatest critics fell silent.

Andrew was always marked out for a sporting career. The captain of Barnard Castle School at rugby, cricket and squash, he toured Portugal and Holland with the school rugby team. At Cambridge University he was a Blue in both rugby and cricket and, after deciding to concentrate on the winter game, graduated to the England ranks via representative outings for Yorkshire and Northern Division. He made his England debut against Romania at Twickenham in January 1985, a match that the hosts won 22-15.

Andrew soon developed a reputation as a safe, if cautious, fly-half with a habit of turning forward possession into points on the board. It may not always have been pretty to watch, particularly against some of the lesser nations, but it was highly effective. Unlucky not to be selected for the British Lions' tour of Australia in 1989, he was called up as a replacement after Paul Dean tore a cartilage in the opening game. Andrew settled in immediately, demonstrating his customary intelligent kicking and solid defence in the provincial matches, and when Craig Chalmers was dropped from the Test side, Andrew stepped in to become the first English fly-half to play in a Lions' Test for 27 years. His partnership with Welshman Robert Jones was instrumental in turning the series around, a personal contribution of a conversion, a penalty and a dropped goal helping defeat

Rob Andrew

Born: Richmond, England, 1963

Country: England

Position: Fly-half

International caps: 71

Clubs: Cambridge University, Nottingham, Wasps, Gordon, Toulouse, Newcastle

Representative honours: British Lions, Barbarians

Australia 19-12 in the second Test.

On the back of the Lions' triumph, Andrew became England's most reliable performer the following season. By 1994 he had added goalkicking to his armoury of tactical kicks and notched a record 30 points with the boot in the 60-19 victory over Canada at Twickenham. The next year was even better as Andrew inspired England to the Grand Slam and a place in the semi-finals of the World Cup. He was also awarded the MBE. That year was expected to be his swansong but he returned for one last appearance against Wales in 1997.

When he retired from international rugby, he was the most capped stand-off in the world and his record of 21 dropped goals was equally unsurpassed. His total of 86 international penalties and 396 points were both England records . . . until Jonny Wilkinson came along. At club level he had played for Nottingham and Wasps (whom he led to the 1990 Championship) as well as spending seasons with the Sydney club Gordon (1986) and Toulouse (1992). In 1995 he became director of rugby at Newcastle.

Rob Andrew can look back on a career in which he confounded the doubters to become one of England's most consistent players. However, a recent newspaper poll of memorable rugby moments put his famous dropped goal against Australia below Erica Roe's Twickenham streak! His former critics no doubt had a quiet chuckle to themselves.

Rob Andrew was the first English fly-half to play in a British Lions test in 27 years

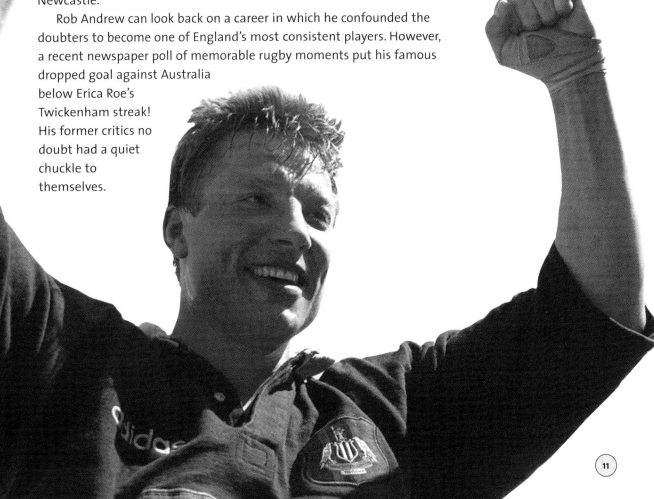

BILL BEAUMONT

Perhaps England's most famous lock, Bill Beaumont started his rugby career as a full-back

Bill Beaumont

Born: Preston, England, 1952

Country: England

Position: Lock

International caps: 34

Clubs: Fylde

Representative honours: Lancashire, British Lions, Barbarians

BILL BEAUMONT

Few players in English rugby are regarded with more affection than William Blackledge Beaumont. When, in 1980, the self-effacing Lancashire lock led England to their first Grand Slam for 23 years, it was proof that nice guys do occasionally win.

Big Bill was a man of contrasts. On the pitch he hit rucks and mauls with the force of a bull elephant; off it he was thoughtful, quietly spoken and blessed with a dry sense of humour. Born in Preston, he was educated at Ellesmere College where he performed with little distinction in the position of full-back. On leaving school he entered the family cotton business and began a long association with Fylde Rugby Club where, switched to a forward role, he began to build up a reputation as an honest, hard-working player who was not afraid to get stuck in. Representative honours for Lancashire were followed in 1975 by the award of a first England cap, against Ireland in Dublin. It ended in a 12-9 defeat but he retained his place for the series in Australia where the new boy was singled out for special attention in the opening Test and was forced to leave the field after being clobbered at the first lineout. Happily he recovered and by the following season had established himself as England's premier jumper at the front of the lineout.

Considered unlucky not have been selected for the 1977 Lions' tour to New Zealand, Beaumont joined the party as a replacement for Moseley lock Nigel Horton and proved a revelation. Forming a formidable partnership with Scotland's Gordon Brown, he played a major role in the second Test win at Christchurch that levelled the series and although the Lions lost the two remaining matches, he had shown himself capable of competing at the highest level. His reward came the following year when he was named England captain.

Beaumont went on to lead his country in 21 matches. His unassuming air rubbed off on his team-mates who responded to his leadership by giving him everything in the quest for victory. Never one for mindless verbal dressing-downs, he found quiet words of encouragement to be infinitely more productive. These qualities reaped a spectacular harvest in season 1979-80. First, by dint of a clever tactical game-plan, he led the North of England to an unexpected 21-9 victory over the All Blacks at Otley; then he captained his beloved Lancashire to the County Championship; and finally he secured that long-awaited Grand Slam for England. It was a close-run thing against Wales, who were leading deep into injury time, until Dusty Hare landed a dramatic touchline penalty. The Welsh might have felt aggrieved but who could begrudge Beaumont his moment of glory, particularly after England had endured so many years of torment?

Having done so much for English team spirit, it was fitting that Beaumont should be given the captaincy of the 1980 Lions for the tour to South Africa – the first Englishman to be awarded that honour since Doug Prentice in 1930. Beaumont's strength, both in the pack and as part of the management team, offered hope of success but in the end a succession of injuries to key players undermined the best-laid plans.

In 1982 Beaumont suffered a nasty head injury while leading Lancashire to victory in the County Championship Final and, acting on medical advice, announced his retirement from the game. Thus his last international was the 9-9 draw at Murrayfield in January of that year.

Bill Beaumont reached an even wider audience in retirement than he ever did as a player, becoming a popular and genial team captain on the long-running panel game *A Question of Sport*. The programme showed precisely why he is held in such high esteem and why his players were prepared to run through brick walls for him back in 1980.

PHIL BENNETT

Down in the Valleys grown men still speak in hushed tones of the Bennett sidestep and swerve. For his gifts were not the sort bestowed upon mere mortals; they came from the gods and were reserved for the chosen few. Who could forget the way he totally wrong-footed three All Blacks at the start of that epic Gareth Edwards try for the Barbarians in 1973? In those glory years of Welsh rugby Phil Bennett's wizardry was one of the star turns.

Yet it did not come easily to the little man from Llanelli. After winning schoolboy and youth international honours, he made his full debut in 1969 when coming on as a substitute for Gerald Davies in Paris, the first Welsh replacement to be capped. With 'The King', Barry John, on the fly-half throne, Bennett spent the next three years being shuffled around from wing to centre to full-back. It was not until John retired in 1972 that Bennett could settle into his favourite position.

Despite a curiously hunched running style, he was as slippery as an

Phil Bennett's amazing career almost ended when he was wrongly diagnosed with a spinal problem

eel, using those twinkling feet and sudden changes of direction to unlock even the most resolute defence. Dodges, feints, jinks, jerks, he had more tricks up his sleeve than a music hall magician. There were few more daunting tasks than stepping into Barry John's boots but Bennett soon won over the Welsh fans, if not always the selectors. A shy, modest man by nature, there was a feeling that he lacked confidence in international matches. That memorable display for the Barbarians won over most of the doubters but no sooner had he cleared one obstacle than another presented itself when, in December of that year, he was diagnosed with spinal trouble in his lower back. He was advised to retire but, fortunately, a second opinion produced a clean bill of health.

He responded to the welcome news with a dazzling display on the Lions' tour of South Africa in 1974, scoring 103 points, the highlight being a brilliant 50-metre try in the second Test in Pretoria as he weaved his way through the Springbok ranks in his own inimitable style. The Lions won three Tests and drew the fourth. Afterwards even the unassuming Bennett reckoned that he had finally arrived on the world stage.

PHIL BENNETT

Nevertheless, he wasn't assured of a place in the Welsh team, being dropped in 1975 and not even being named as a replacement for the first match in the 1975-76 International Championship. Furthermore, unemployment caused him to consider emigrating. Everything was resolved, however, and he regained his place to become an essential ingredient in Wales' hat-trick of Triple Crowns. In 1977 he succeeded Mervyn Davies as captain of his country and in the same year he became only the second Welshman to skipper a Lions' tour when he led the team to New Zealand. It was not a happy experience. Bennett's game suffered under the burden of captaincy and the series ended in a 3-1 defeat. Some critics even questioned whether he was worth his place before the final Test, even though he managed to score 112 points on the tour. He retired from international rugby the following year, his confidence having perhaps taken one knock too many.

Yet there were times when Bennett's fervent patriotism instilled in him all the confidence in the world. Before Wales met England at Cardiff in 1977 he delivered a truly inspirational pre-match team talk. 'Look at what these f*****s have done to Wales,' he raged. 'They've taken our coal, our water and our steel. What have they given us? Absolutely nothing. We've been exploited, raped, controlled and punished by the English – and that's who you're playing this afternoon!' Given such a build-up, it was no surprise that Wales went out and won 14-9 *en route* to another Triple Crown.

Phil Bennett

Born: Felin Foel, Wales, 1948

Country: Wales

Position: Wing, centre, fly-half

International caps: 29

Clubs: Llanelli

Representative honours: British Lions, Barbarians

SERGE BLANCO

SERGE BLANCO

The date: 13 June 1987. The venue: the Concord Oval, Sydney. The occasion: the semi-final of the inaugural Rugby World Cup. Hosts Australia had swept their way imperiously to that stage, brushing aside England, the USA and Japan in their pool games and amassing 108 points in the process. When Ireland were crushed 33-15 in the quarter-final, everyone in the southern hemisphere was relishing the prospect of a dream final between the Wallabies and the All Blacks. Only France stood in Australia's way but their route to the last four had been a fitful, stuttering affair – a draw with Scotland followed by unimpressive, if ultimately emphatic, victories over weak opposition. Furthermore, Australia had beaten the French 27-14 on the same ground only a year earlier. David Campese and co. were supremely confident of a repeat result.

But France had other ideas and a tense, tight affair swung first one way and then the other until the scores were locked at 24-24 with just a minute remaining. The French launched one last desperate raid deep into Australian territory but the move appeared to have broken down 20 metres out with exhausted bodies scattered across the turf. Then, just as the Australian fans were about to breathe a collective sigh of relief, the French No. 8, Laurent Rodriguez – 'The Bull of Dax' – fed full-back Serge Blanco who was steaming up in support. As Blanco sprinted to the corner past flailing defenders, Australia's hopes appeared to go with him. History records that France were well beaten in the final but the showcase tournament had been treated to a moment of Blanco magic.

By then rugby fans in Britain were all too familiar with Blanco's graceful yet powerful running, his smooth acceleration, devastating changes of pace, exquisite handling and timing and, above all, his clinical finishing. And he did it all with the style and flair that the French demand from their top sportsmen despite smoking 40 cigarettes a day and rarely bothering to train.

Progressing through the French junior ranks, the Caracas-born Blanco made his full international debut at full-back in 1980 against South Africa in Pretoria, a match played in defiance of the sports boycott of that country. Three weeks later he was part of the French team beaten 15-0 in Romania – the first time France had failed to score in an international since 1964. Blanco survived the fallout but was switched to the wing where he played in three of the matches in the 1981 Grand Slam before being permitted to revert to his natural

Serge Blanco

Born: Caracas, Venezuela, 1958

Country: France

Position: Full-back, wing

International caps: 93

Clubs: Biarritz

Representative honours: Barbarians

position of full-back. Although Blanco was a supremely talented athlete, this chopping and changing was a puzzle. Gareth Edwards wrote at the time: 'Blanco is so gifted, and possessed of such good judgement, that all he needs is to be given the number fifteen shirt and to be allowed a free rein to innovate and extemporise.'

It was at full-back that he really blossomed (his 81 Test caps in that position is a French record) and in 1997 he inspired his country to another Grand Slam. Despite his heroics against Australia, the World Cup eluded 'the Biarritz Bombshell' and when France were knocked out by England in the quarter-finals of the 1991 tournament, he decided to take his leave of the international stage that he had graced so effortlessly for the previous 11 years. His last first-class game was for his club, Biarritz, but it ended in defeat to Toulon in the final of the French club competition. A double disappointment was an unjust way to end such a glittering career. He finished with 93 Test caps (a French record until overtaken by Philippe Sella) and 38 Test tries, a total which remains unsurpassed in French rugby. It may well be beaten one day but the memories of Serge Blanco will surely remain forever.

Serge Blanco had a natural athleticism seemingly unhampered by smoking 40 cigarettes a day

Widely regarded as one of the world's greatest No. 8s, Zinzan Brooke only became the All Black's first choice in that position at the age of 30

ZINZAN BROOKE

With the build of a forward but the skills and flair of a back, Zinzan Brooke is widely acknowledged as the most complete No.8 to have played in world rugby. If proof of his all-round ability were needed, it came during the semi-final of the 1995 World Cup when he kicked an outrageous dropped goal in New Zealand's 45-29 hammering of England – one of three he would kick in Test matches.

He entered first-class rugby in 1986 as Murray Zinzan Brooke but swapped his names by deed poll to reflect his family history. After impressing for New Zealand colts, his strength and mobility caught the eye of the national selectors the following year while playing for New Zealand sevens and consequently he was chosen for the 1987 World Cup squad. Replacing Michael Jones, he made his international debut on the openside flank in the pool match against Argentina at Wellington, scoring the first of his 41 tries for his country.

Brooke toured Japan at the end of 1987 and Australia the next year but didn't play another Test until 1989 when he again replaced Jones against Argentina. This set the pattern for much of his early career, playing as an all-purpose loose forward who filled in occasionally for established back-rowers such as Jones, Alan Whetton and Wayne Shelford. Even when Shelford was dropped after the two-Test series against Scotland in 1990 and Brooke took over at No. 8, he did not become an automatic choice, his appearances restricted by niggling injuries and selectors' indifference. Although he did play in five of the matches at the 1991 World Cup, he continued to spend too much time on the reserves bench and it was only relatively late in his career that he finally made the No. 8 spot his own.

The breakthrough came in 1995 when Brooke emerged as a key member of his country's exciting World Cup team. Following a 145-17 massacre of Japan, the New Zealanders swept aside Scotland and England with a brand of thrilling, attacking rugby, only to lose 15-12 in the final to hosts South Africa. Brooke was at last a regular fixture, cementing his place in 1996 with five international tries and helping the All Blacks to gain a degree of revenge over the Springboks. Brooke's try in the first Test at Durban enabled New Zealand to win 23-19 and he did even better in the second Test at Pretoria, scoring a try and landing a crucial dropped goal as the All Blacks clinched the series with a hard-fought 33-26 victory. He scored two more tries against Australia in his fiftieth Test in 1997 to set a new world record of seventeen for the number of Test tries by a forward.

Despite being appointed captain of Auckland when Sean Fitzpatrick was made skipper of the All Blacks, Brooke yearned to try his luck abroad. He nearly joined the Sydney club, Manly, and was on the verge of going to play in Japan until commercial deals were struck to persuade him to stay in New Zealand. When he eventually announced his retirement from international rugby at the end of the All Blacks' 1997 tour to Britain and Ireland (his last match was the 26-26 draw with England at Twickenham), he joined Harlequins, first as player, then as coach. He stepped down from that role in 2001.

Zinzan Brooke scored over 150 tries in first-class rugby, including 42 for his country. Many of the rest were pushovers at the base of the powerful Auckland pack but that fact should not detract from his unique versatility, which prompted New Zealand coach John Hart to suggest that there would never be another player like 'Zinny'. In 1999 *Rugby World* magazine voted Brooke the second best No. 8 of all time behind Mervyn Davies. Plenty in the southern hemisphere believe the positions should be reversed.

Zinzan Brooke

Born: Waiuku, New Zealand, 1965

Country: New Zealand

Position: No. 8

International caps: 58

Clubs: Auckland Marist, Auckland Blues, Harlequins

Representative honours: Auckland, Barbarians

OLLIE CAMPBELL

OLLIE CAMPBELL

With a calculated swing of his trusty right foot, flame-haired Ollie Campbell kicked himself into the Irish record books between 1976 and 1984. The Dublin-born fly-half set an Irish record on the 1979 tour to Australia by scoring 60 points, nineteen of them in the Brisbane Test, thereby establishing an Irish record for points in a match against Australia. In 1982 his 21 points against Scotland in Dublin created an individual Irish points-scoring record against any opposition and he equalled that mark at Lansdowne Road the following year, this time with England on the receiving end of the Campbell boot. His six penalties in that Scotland match were also an Irish record and his career total of 54 penalties comfortably outstripped Tom Kiernan's target, although it has since been passed by Michael Kiernan, Eric Elwood and David Humphreys. Similarly Campbell's haul of 217 points in Test matches set a new Irish record until being overhauled by the aforementioned trio.

Campbell was the driving force behind Ireland's Five Nations successes in the early Eighties yet was by no means an overnight sensation. The Old Belvedere fly-half had made his international debut back in 1976 in the 20-10 defeat to Australia in Dublin but had then fallen from favour at the expense of his great rival, Tony Ward. Rather like the Andrew/Barnes situation for England a decade later, Ireland were in the enviable position of having two outstanding fly-halves of contrasting styles. Each brought something different to the party. Ward was fleet of foot, a mercurial individualist, capable of moments of sheer brilliance that thrilled the Irish crowds. Campbell, on the other hand, was a more reliable performer, a safe kicker, good at covering and arguably better at linking with his threequarters. Given the nod, Ward gleefully accepted his chance, his early performances leading him to be acclaimed the best fly-half in the world. However the debate about the relative merits of the two players continued to rage in the bars of Ireland and in 1979 the Campbell camp were rewarded for their patience when their man was selected for the tour of Australia.

Determined to make the most of his opportunity now that it had finally arrived, Campbell did well Down Under and carried his form over into the 1980 Championship, as a result of which he was chosen for the Lions' tour of South Africa. But when Campbell suffered hamstring problems and fellow fly-half Gareth Davies injured his shoulder, Ward was flown out as a replacement and promptly made his mark by scoring 18 points in the first Test at Cape Town – a record for a Lion in

Ollie Campbell

Born: Dublin, Eire, 1954

Country: Ireland

Position: Fly-half

International caps: 22

Clubs: Old Belvedere

Representative honours: British Lions, Barbarians

an international. Campbell regained his fitness towards the end of the tour and played in the final two Tests, demonstrating his place-kicking ability to head the Lions' points-scoring list with 60.

In 1982 Campbell helped Ireland to their first Triple Crown for 33 years. Now firmly established as first choice over Ward, he began to add a new dimension to his game, running at the opposition with great flair to set up chances for his colleagues. He also emerged as a shrewd tactical kicker, able to dictate play and find touch with uncanny precision. The 1983 Five Nations title was shared with France and Campbell's consistency and new-found attacking play earned him a second Lions' tour, to New Zealand. He arrived with a glowing reputation but sadly failed to live up to it, the All Blacks restricting his kicking opportunities and harassing him at every opportunity. Four Test defeats later and Campbell was held partly responsible for the indifferent displays, accused of failing to galvanise the back line.

After being on the losing side against France and Wales in 1984, company director Campbell was forced to withdraw from the remainder of the Five Nations through illness. It was a downbeat end to a short but explosive international career.

In his relatively short international career, Ollie Campbell set several Irish points-scoring records

DAVID CAMPESE

David Campese won his hundredth cap against Italy, where he also played for Milan

David Campese

Born: Queanbeyan, Australia, 1962

Country: Australia

Position: Wing

International caps: 101

Clubs: Queanbeyan, Randwick, Milan

Province/District: New South Wales, Barbarians

DAVID CAMPESE

David Campese not only played a good game, he talked one too. Indeed the New South Wales winger has become almost as well known for expressing his high opinion of his own abilities and his low opinion of others' as for his remarkable exploits on the pitch, which saw him become the first Australian player to reach a century of caps.

There was no sitting on the fence with 'Campo'. Rugby fans either loved him or hated him. He was brash, outspoken, selfish, unpredictable but also capable of flashes of sublime brilliance that could win matches. When Campese was on song, he didn't need team-mates; he could do it all by himself . . . and he usually did. His trademark move was 'the Goosestep', an exaggerated step that fooled opponents into thinking he was slowing down when in fact he was speeding up. He was such a spontaneous player that opponents had no idea what he was about to do next. Then again, neither did he. As his Wallaby captain Nick Farr-Jones once remarked: 'Sometimes even Campo's brain doesn't know where his feet are taking him.'

He could delight and infuriate in equal measures. At the height of his powers in 1989 he was responsible for one of the most calamitous blunders in modern rugby. With the series against the British Lions tied at one apiece and the Wallabies hanging on to a slender advantage in the Sydney decider, Campese threw a suicidal goal-line pass to full-back Greg Martin instead of kicking to touch. Lions' winger Ieuan Evans gleefully capitalised on Campese's folly to score the try that helped the Lions take the series. An unrepentant Campese was pilloried in the press by ex-internationals and even by an electronics company which used a photograph of the error to advertise a new video recorder with the slogan 'Now you can watch Campo cock up as often as you like!'

Controversy was nothing new to Campese. The boy from Queanbeyan, near Canberra, made his international debut against the All Blacks at Christchurch in 1982 where his opponent was the legendary Stu Wilson. Campese had wound Wilson up before the match by claiming never to have heard of him. New Zealand won 23-16 but Campese had the satisfaction of outfoxing Wilson on a number of occasions and scoring an opportunist try late on. After starring in Australia's 1984 Grand Slam over the home nations, Campese racked up try after try on his way to a world record career total of 64 in Test matches. The highspot was inspiring his country to victory in the 1991 World Cup, the semi-final against New Zealand being considered his finest game at international level. He scored a typical try early on and then, with an instinctive flicked pass, sent Tim Horan over for the winner. Before the final with England, Campese put his mouth into overdrive, blasting them for boring, unimaginative play and insisting: 'I wouldn't play for England if you paid me.' Significantly, England abandoned their usual reliance on Rob Andrew's boot in favour of a more open game. The change in tactics suited Australia better than England who went under 12-6, Campese making a crucial interception to deny Rory Underwood. The aberration of two years earlier had been forgotten . . . well almost.

As advancing years began to diminish his blistering pace, he introduced fresh ways of humiliating opponents. A few gave him a taste of his own medicine. Before the 1993 Bledisloe Cup clash, New Zealand's giant winger Vai'iga Tuigimala sent Campese a photograph of himself performing the haka with a covering note: 'To my friend Campo. This is the top half. You'll see the rest on Sunday.' Tuigimala was as good as word, powering the All Blacks to a 25-10 triumph.

Campese finally called it a day in 1996 shortly after winning his hundredth cap against Italy, his ancestral home. The rugby field was a much quieter – and poorer – place without him.

WILL CARLING

No British rugby player has ever enjoyed such a high profile as Will Carling . . . although perhaps 'enjoyed' isn't quite the word. After all, this is the man who was sacked from the England captaincy for describing the Rugby Football Union committee as '57 old farts', was alleged to have had a dangerous liaison with the Princess of Wales (a rumour which appeared to precipitate a divorce from his TV presenter wife Julia), and was later dubbed a 'love rat' by the tabloid press for deserting his fiancée and eleven-month-old child. Understandably, the headlines made by these off-field distractions have tended to obliterate Carling's playing achievements. As England's youngest captain for 57 years, he led them out of the doldrums to three Grand Slams and a World Cup Final. His critics argued that England were boring to watch and that Carling himself was lucky to be surrounded by so many good players, but his leadership ability was consistently astute and frequently innovative.

Born in Bradford-on-Avon, Wiltshire, Carling captained England Schoolboys as an eighteen-year-old and went on to represent the Barbarians and Harlequins before making his full England debut against France in January 1988. A few months later and still relatively unknown, the 22-year-old army captain was asked by coach Geoff Cooke to lead the team against Australia at Twickenham in place of Bristol scrum-half Richard Harding. It was a considerable gamble by Cooke but one that paid off immediately as England triumphed 28-19. However, shin splints forced Carling to miss the 1989 Lions' tour to Australia and less than a year later Scotland stole the Grand Slam from under England's noses with a dramatic 13-7 victory at Murrayfield.

Devising a game plan around powerful forwards such as Wade Dooley, Dean Richards and Mike Teague, Carling and Cooke built a team that would become the dominant force in northern hemisphere rugby. The disappointment of 1990 was quickly forgotten when, 12 months later, Carling led England to their first Grand Slam for 11 years and, for good measure, to the final of the World Cup where they gave Australia a real fright before going down 12-6. In 1992 he skippered England to a second successive Grand Slam, the previous England captain to have achieved back-to-back Grand Slams having been Wavell Wakefield as long ago as 1924. Even if the critics bemoaned England's lack of imaginative play, Carling, it seemed, could do no wrong.

A further Grand Slam followed in 1995 but then Carling, who had never enjoyed the healthiest of relationships with sections of the RFU,

GREAT RUGBY HEROES

WILL CARLING

Will Carling was England's youngest captain in over half a century and led the team to three Grand Slams

made his injudicious remarks in a TV interview and was promptly relieved of the captaincy. With the World Cup looming and nobody willing to take Carling's place, the RFU were forced into an embarrassing U-turn, and, after making a public apology, he was given his job back. Given the humiliation inflicted on England in the semi-final by Jonah Lomu, Carling probably wished he had stayed at home.

He did eventually step down as captain following the 1996 Triple Crown with the remarkable record of 44 wins from the 59 Tests in which he had led his country. Confounding those who maintained that he was not worth his place in the side solely as a player, he continued to be selected as England centre for another 12 months, retiring after a 34-13 triumph in Cardiff had clinched yet another Triple Crown.

If Carling hoped for an anonymous life in club rugby, he was wrong. He quit after falling out with Harlequins' coach Andy Keast and was only persuaded to return to The Stoop 13 months later when All Blacks John Gallagher and Zinzan Brooke took over coaching duties. But when Carling tried to promote his testimonial season, he discovered to his cost that the revelations about his colourful private life had turned public opinion against him. England's most successful rugby captain had become an outcast. And all for the love of several good women.

Will Carling

Born: Bradford-on-Avon, England, 1965

Country: England

Position: Centre

International caps: 72

Clubs: Durham University, Harlequins

Representative honours: British Lions, Barbarians

DON CLARKE

The *New Zealand Rugby Almanack* wrote of Don Clarke's first-class debut for Waikato province in 1951: 'While Don Clarke rendered fine service to his union, he appeared rather too cumbersome to be able to reach much farther than inter-union standard.' How Clarke would make the writer eat his words, going on to score 207 points in Test matches for the All Blacks and earn such a reputation for fearless goal-kicking that to New Zealand fans he was known simply as 'The Boot', the finest full-back of his generation.

Adversity was nothing new to Clarke. As a ten-year-old he hiked twelve miles to play in a primary school trial, only to arrive too late to participate. Indeed, the local schools weren't keen on him playing rugby or football. Due to his huge physique (by the age of thirteen he weighed thirteen stone and could throw a cricket ball 100 metres), his school decided it was safer if he played netball instead! However, he regularly took part in club rugby, representing an under-eighteen side when he was just twelve, and as soon as he left school he clinched the coveted Ranfurly Shield for Waikato by kicking two huge goals from the mud of Rugby Park, Whangerei. Even so, some advisers suggested he become a forward but his father told him to stick to his ambition of being a full-back.

Don was one of five rugby-playing brothers (the quintet once appeared together for Waikato in 1961) and it was his siblings who helped him through another crisis when injury and loss of form threatened to end his career almost before it had started. After undergoing operations on both knees, the 6ft 2in, 17st 7lb Clarke was back to his best by 1956 and made his Test debut at Christchurch mid-way through the series with South Africa. After just two minutes he landed a 45-metre penalty before 51,000 hushed fans and went on to score eight points in New Zealand's 17-10 triumph. He scored eight more points in the next Test to establish the full-back position as his own, missing just one more Test over the next eight years – and that was due to injury.

The Springboks had discovered what other international teams would soon learn – that Clarke was deceptively quick, strong in the tackle and a good handler, the last a result of his grounding in cricket (he was a lively fast bowler who represented Waikato, Auckland and Northern Districts). But above all he was a magnificent kicker, using his brute strength and basic toe-kicking style to launch penalties and conversions from seemingly impossible distances. He broke the hearts of the British Lions in Dunedin in 1959 by kicking what was then a world record six penalties to wipe out the tourists' four tries and edge the New Zealanders home by a single point. To rub salt into the wounds, Clarke scored the try that won the second Test at Wellington. The British never forgave him.

The following year it was again South Africa's turn to be on the receiving end of 'The Boot'. Singled out for rough treatment by the Springboks, Clarke responded by kicking a colossal 60-metre penalty and then landing a nail-biting conversion as the All Blacks clawed themselves back from the brink of defeat to snatch an 11-11 draw in the third Test at Bloemfontein. New Zealand lost the series but Clarke's place in All Black folklore was assured.

His final Test was a 20-5 defeat to Australia at Wellington in 1964. He was all set to face the Springboks once more when the troublesome knees flared up. He played in a total of 89 games for the All Blacks, compiling 781 points.

Upon retirement, he coached Waikato school representative sides before emigrating to South Africa in the 1970s where he set up a tree-felling business. Seriously injured in a car crash in 1997, he was diagnosed with melanoma in March 2002 and died nine months later.

GREAT RUGBY HEROES

DON CLARKE

Don Clarke achieved incredible distance with his toe-poke kicking style

Don Clarke

Born: Pihama, New Zealand, 1933 (d. 2002)

Country: New Zealand

Position: Full-back

International caps: 31

Clubs: Kereone, Morinsville

Representative honours: Waikato, North Island

GREAT RUGBY HEROES

FRAN COTTON

FRAN COTTON

The cornerstone of England's pack in the 1970s, Fran Cotton gave everything to the cause. For nine years he toiled away, often in vain, as England struggled to put together a competitive unit, until finally in 1980 he had something to celebrate as part of Bill Beaumont's Grand Slam team. The reward was richly deserved.

Yet Cotton could so easily have been lost to Rugby League. Raised in the League hotbed of Wigan, his father and brother were both professionals with Warrington and Cotton's own boyhood heroes were League legends Billy Boston and Bev Risman. However, Cotton was converted to the 15-a-side game at Newton-le-Willows Grammar School and while playing for Loughborough Colleges (where he was training as a PE teacher) his acumen in the front row alerted the England selectors. He won his first cap against Scotland in 1971 and proceeded to finish on the losing side in his first five internationals. It was not until a 14-6

victory over France at Twickenham in 1973 that he tasted success for his country. In the meantime he had, however, made his mark on world rugby by leading the North to a memorable victory over the 1972 All Blacks at Otley – the first time that an English province had beaten the New Zealanders.

The 1973 win against France heralded something of a mini-revival for England and Cotton was very much a key component in this change of fortune. At 6ft 2in tall and weighing over 17 stone, he possessed all the physical attributes for a prop and was equally comfortable on the tight-head as on the loose. Extraordinarily fit and technically gifted, his experience and scrummaging skills earned him a place on the 1974 Lions' tour to South Africa as understudy loose-head to Scotland's Ian McLauchlan but when injuries took their toll among the forwards, the versatile Cotton was able to win a place on the tight-head for the first Test, a position he retained for the rest of the series. Without doubt it was the forwards' dominance of the Springboks that laid the foundations for the Lions' Test record of three wins and a draw – the first time South Africa had lost a full-scale Test series at home that century.

Back home, England's brief upturn had come to a grinding halt but Cotton was still chosen for the 1977 Lions' tour to New Zealand. He struggled early on and was overlooked for the first Test (a 16-12 defeat in Wellington) but returned for the second where, in the role of loose-head, he made a telling contribution to help the Lions square the series. With Cotton to the fore, the Lions' forwards continued to revel in the atrocious conditions created by one of New Zealand's wettest-ever winters. However, in the last two Tests forward power was wasted by the backs who became uncharacteristically bogged down, allowing New Zealand to wrap up the series.

At 33, Cotton sampled the highlight of his England career with the 1980 Grand Slam, forming a powerhouse partnership with Peter Wheeler and Phil Blakeway. But later that year in South Africa, while on his third Lions' tour, he suffered a suspected heart attack during the match with the Federation XV and had to be stretchered off. It was feared that his playing days were over but his determination to fight his way back to the top was revealed when he made an emotional return against Wales in Cardiff the following year. It proved a false dawn and a leg injury soon forced him to retire.

Fran Cotton has retained his links with rugby, firstly as a businessman (his Cotton Traders company has supplied the kit to many of the world's national teams) and secondly as a manager, being placed in charge of the Lions' 1997 tour to South Africa.

An unlikely exponent of the scrum half's dive pass, prop Fran Cotton displays his versatility

Fran Cotton

Born: Wigan, England, 1947

Country: England

Position: Prop

International caps: 31

Clubs: Loughborough Colleges, Coventry, Sale

Representative honours: British Lions, Barbarians

GERALD DAVIES

GERALD DAVIES

With devastating acceleration and a perfectly disguised sidestep, Gerald Davies was one of the great entertainers during the Golden Age of Welsh rugby. Over a 12-year period from 1966 to 1978, his dazzling footwork baffled and bewildered many of the world's foremost players, bringing him 20 tries on international duty to create a Welsh record that he shared at the time with his Cardiff colleague Gareth Edwards.

In company with Edwards, Phil Bennett, J.J. Williams and J.P.R. Williams, Davies formed the nucleus of the outstanding Wales back division – one of the most potent combinations seen in the history of international rugby. He was at his best on the Lions' 1971 tour to New Zealand where he used his verve and swerve to run in three tries in the triumphant Test series.

Thomas Gerald Reames Davies was born in Llansaint and attended Queen Elizabeth Grammar School in Carmarthen. As a teenager he was capped by the Welsh Secondary Schools before going on to qualify as a schoolmaster at Loughborough. He made his full international debut in 1966 as a centre and his attacking style made such an impact that he was chosen for the 1968 Lions' tour of South Africa. Although restricted by injuries to just nine appearances on the tour, his performance in the third Test at Cape Town (which the Lions lost 11-6) gave hope of better things to come. He returned home with a new-found reputation as Britain's most creative threequarter and certainly the only mid-field player capable of breaking through the South African defence.

In the autumn of 1968 he went up to Cambridge to read English. A quiet, thoughtful young man, he revelled in the academic atmosphere but still found time for international rugby. The following year, while on tour with Wales in New Zealand and Australia, he was asked to play at wing-threequarter – a position which allowed him to utilise his speed to maximum effect. But he didn't just charge around like a headless chicken. He timed his runs intelligently and very rarely dropped a pass, proving equally effective at scoring tries over long and short distances. A 50-metre run or a close-range burst into the corner, they all came the same to Davies as he quickly developed into one of the game's most lethal finishers. More often than not he would surge into space on the end of an intricate passing move, shimmy past a couple of defenders as if they were statues and touch down in the blink of an eye. He managed to make the seemingly impossible look routine.

He withdrew from the 1970 Welsh squad in order to concentrate on

Gerald Davies

Born: Llansaint, Wales, 1945

Country: Wales

Position: Centre, wing

International caps: 46

Clubs: Cambridge University, Cardiff, London Welsh

Province/District: British Lions, Barbarians

his finals but he returned, rejuvenated, next season to score five tries as Wales won the Grand Slam. Then came that New Zealand tour with the Lions. The series level at 1-1, it was Davies who squeezed in at the corner early in the third Test at Wellington to set the Lions on the road to a decisive 13-3 win. He also showed his mettle in the provincial game against Hawke's Bay whose tactics seemed to revolve around putting Davies and some of his team-mates in the nearest hospital. But first they had to catch him. Never once losing his cool, he responded to the hosts' brutality by rattling in four spectacular tries, leaving his opponents lumbering in his wake.

Davies continued to be a mainstay of Wales's domination of the 1970s, which brought them a share of the Five Nations in 1973, outright victory in 1975, Triple Crowns in 1976, 1977 and 1978 and further Grand Slams in 1976 and 1978. Gerald Davies retired that year as his country's most capped threequarter and has never been adequately replaced. Then again, he was a tough act to follow.

His England opposite number, David Duckham, once said of Davies: 'You know exactly what he's going to do. He's going to come off his right foot at great speed. You also know there isn't a blind thing you can do about it!'

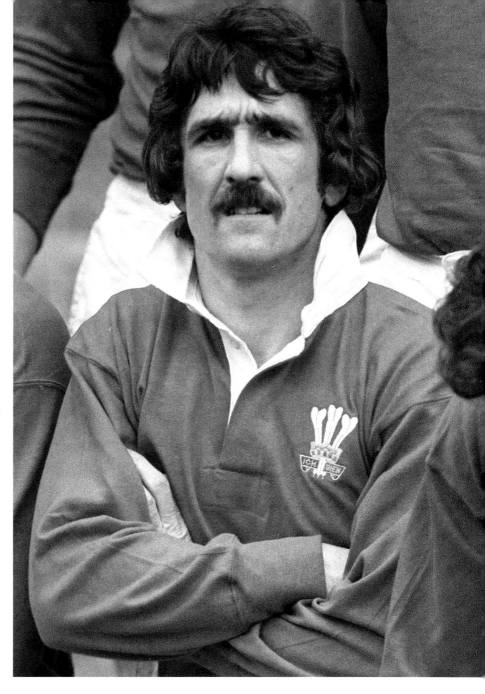

Gerald Davies made the first of his 46 appearances for Wales in 1966 against Australia in Cardiff

JONATHAN DAVIES

JONATHAN DAVIES

The most exciting talent to emerge in Wales since the 1970s, Jonathan Davies inspired Wales to a Triple Crown victory in 1988

Welsh rugby was in the doldrums in 1985. The country's previous Five Nations title had been six years earlier but to fans raised on the heady days of Edwards, Bennett, J.P.R. and co., it might as well have been sixty. What they needed above all was a new hero. Then a young fly-half from Llanelli strode onto the international stage with a swagger that suggested he would be the answer to Welsh prayers for many years to come. Almost overnight, abandoned hopes and dreams were resurrected on the back of this supremely talented 22-year-old. But no sooner had he arrived in a blaze of glory than he was off again, disillusioned with the state of the national game. With him, he took the dreams of thousands of Welshmen.

Born in Trimsaran, Carmarthenshire, Jonathan Davies recorded his senior debut for Neath where he made his name as an intelligent player whose brain moved as fast as his feet. Seeking drastic measures to breathe fire back into the Welsh dragon, the selectors called the youngster up to face England at Cardiff on 20 April 1985. England were also going through a transitional period and were ill-prepared to deal with the young master wearing the red number ten shirt so immortalised by the likes of Barry John and Phil Bennett. If the burden of wearing the revered fly-half jersey preyed on Davies at all, it certainly didn't show. Demonstrating remarkable composure, imagination, vision, an electrifying burst of pace and magical handling skills, he crowned his debut with a try and a dropped goal to steer Wales to a memorable 24-15 win. As far as those success-starved supporters were concerned, Wales were back.

At first the omens were good. Six months after his debut, Davies featured in an emphatic 40-3 win over Fiji and kept his place for the 1986 Five Nations Championship, playing in every match. People outside Wales were starting to sit up and take notice, realising that the England game wasn't simply a case of beginner's luck, all the more so when Davies played a pivotal role in his country's march to the semi-finals of the inaugural World Cup. After topping their group, winning all three games against Ireland, Canada and Tonga, Wales disposed of England 16-3 in the quarter-finals to set up a clash with eventual champions New Zealand. Wales were duly thrashed 49-6 but Davies inspired them to one last effort and they managed to edge out Australia 22-21 in the third place match.

The third best rugby country in the world won the Triple Crown in 1988 with Davies again playing a pivotal role. His running game tore

England to shreds and his two dropped goals secured victory over Scotland in Cardiff. In the same year he kicked his new club, Llanelli, to victory against his old one in the Welsh Cup Final.

Everything in the Welsh garden appeared rosy until the team's shortcomings were cruelly exposed on the tour to New Zealand, resulting in 52-3 and 54-9 Test humiliations, although Davies, the one player to stand out in the Welsh line-up, did score an astounding 90-metre try in that second Test. Davies returned with ideas as to how Welsh rugby should develop but when his suggestions were ignored and he was publicly criticised by management following a defeat to Romania, he decided to swap codes and join Widnes Rugby League Club for £225,000.

He enjoyed seven outstanding years in Rugby League, becoming the only man to have captained a national side in both disciplines. With the advent of professionalism, he was lured back to Union and Cardiff in 1995 and went on to win five more caps. His last appearance for Wales was against England on 15 March 1999. It was the final game to be played at Cardiff Arms Park and, fittingly, it was Jonathan Davies who scored the last points there.

Jonathan Davies

Born: Trimsaran, Wales, 1962

Country: Wales

Position: Fly-half

International caps: 32

Clubs: Neath, Llanelli, Widnes (RL), Cardiff

Representative honours: Barbarians

Mervyn Davies

Born: Swansea, Wales, 1946

Country: Wales

Position: No. 8

International caps: 38

Clubs: London Welsh, Swansea

Representative honours: British Lions, Barbarians

MERVYN DAVIES

'Merv the Swerve' was the outstanding No. 8 in world rugby during the early 1970s. In match after match that familiar white headband could be seen rising at the back of the lineout to feed quality ball to his colleagues. Even the mighty All Blacks could not contend with his supremacy, which laid the groundwork for the Lions' 3-1 victory in the 1971 series. As such a giant of the game, it was doubly tragic that Davies was forced to retire early following a life-threatening brain haemorrhage.

The Swansea beanpole gave little indication of future glories in his younger days. A modest schoolboy record led to him turning out for the lower ranks of London Welsh while he taught in the south-east. However he quickly worked his way up to the first XV and then, with almost indecent haste, the 22-year-old was summoned to the Welsh line-up for the 1969 international with Scotland at Murrayfield. A winning start (17-3) was just a taste of things to come as he kept his place for the next seven years.

Davies was not the biggest No. 8 in history but his lack of bulk allowed him to be more mobile than some of his counterparts. Even so, he wasn't blessed with a notable turn of foot but his clever reading of the game and ability to anticipate situations – both in attack and defence — compensated for this one deficiency. Gareth Edwards once described him as 'a sort of rugby-playing octopus: a participant who gathered in all around him – ball and players – and gave the game shape and coherence.'

MERVYN DAVIES

Having performed consistently throughout 1971, his place on the tour to New Zealand was a foregone conclusion. He played 13 games on tour, including all four Tests, and repeatedly outwitted the All Blacks in the lineout. With a typically colourful turn of phrase, New Zealand captain Colin Meads conceded that Davies 'had us donkey-licked' at the tail of the lineout. Deprived of their traditional superiority in that area, the New Zealanders struggled to contain the Lions' backs and paid a heavy price.

With his tireless tackling and assured handling, Davies's stature grew by the season. At club level he turned his hometown club, Swansea, into one of the most successful in Welsh rugby while in internationals he formed a solid partnership with Edwards who admitted that having someone like Davies around made life so much easier for a scrum-half.

Davies went on a second Lions' tour – to South Africa – in 1974 but faced stiff competition for his place from England's Andy Ripley who possessed a distinctly sharper turn of foot. However superb outings against Orange Free State and Northern Transvaal, topped by crucial tries in both games, ensured that Davies remained first choice for the opening Test. He responded to the vote of confidence with a succession of dominating displays that allowed the Lions to be victorious once more on foreign soil.

In 1975 he was asked to captain a reshaped Welsh side. By mixing old hands and young blood, he built a team that won the Championship that year and went on to claim the Grand Slam 12 months later.

He was expected to crown his career by captaining the 1977 Lions to New Zealand but then tragedy struck in the semi-finals of the 1976 Welsh Cup. The gentle giant who had never performed a malicious act on the rugby field suffered a brain haemorrhage, which not only ended his playing days but very nearly ended his life.

Forced to retire in the wake of major surgery, Mervyn Davies is still highly thought of wherever rugby is played. He left behind an excellent record as Welsh captain (only one defeat in nine games) and the achievement of being the most capped Welsh forward until Graham Price passed his total several seasons later.

Mervyn Davies received the OBE at Buckingham Palace in 1976 when comedians Morecambe and Wise were also honoured

Wade Dooley

Born: Warrington, England, 1957

Country: England

Position: Lock

International caps: 55

Clubs: Preston Grasshoppers

Representative honours: The North, British Lions, Barbarians

WADE DOOLEY

Success on the rugby field came relatively late in life to Wade Dooley. But the 6ft 8in Blackpool policeman – known to friend and foe alike as 'the Blackpool Tower' – made up for lost time by establishing himself as a pivotal member of the England pack under Geoff Cooke. He excelled in the middle of the lineout where his height, athleticism, confident ball handling and work-rate invariably enabled England to dominate that area of the game.

Born in Warrington, Dooley played league until discovering union in his late teens. He joined the unfashionable Preston Grasshoppers where, under the tutelage of coach Dick Greenwood, he acquired a formidable reputation in the north-west, leading eventually to a belated first international cap at the age of 27 in 1985 – a 22-15 victory over Romania at Twickenham. As part of an unsettled England side, Dooley initially struggled to make an impact, his cause not helped by the occasional bout of indiscipline, which saw him receive a one-match

ban following a violent altercation with Wales in 1987. The irony was not lost that a policeman had difficulty obeying the laws of the game.

His fortunes began to change in 1988 when fellow policeman Paul Ackford was recruited to the England line-up and together the pair formed an outstanding second-row partnership. Dooley's reward was a call-up for the Lions' tour of Australia in 1989. Although Welshman Rob Norster was selected for the First Test, defeat in that match necessitated changes and Dooley stepped in to supply the steely determination that brought victory in the second Test (19-12) and the third (19-18) to clinch a memorable series for the Lions. In total, Dooley played in seven matches on that tour, finishing on the winning side on every occasion.

He continued the good work in the 1990 Five Nations Championship as England's blend of youth and experience promised to carry all before them, only to fall at the final hurdle against Scotland – a game in which Dooley equalled Bill Beaumont's England record for the number of appearances at lock. However, success was just around the corner and the elusive Grand Slam was captured the following year. After sustaining a broken hand playing against Queensland on the tour of Australia, Dooley returned to play in the 1991 World Cup, anxious to make amends for England's disappointment of four years previously. Although England lost narrowly to Australia in the 1991 final, Dooley's performances marked him down as one of the most accomplished locks in the history of English rugby.

Continuing to improve with age, he helped England to a second successive Grand Slam in 1992 (in the process scoring his first England try, against Wales at Twickenham) and was chosen to tour New Zealand with the Lions in 1993. Sadly Dooley's tour was marred by the death of his father and, after returning home for the funeral, he was mysteriously refused permission to rejoin the Lions party. When Martin Johnson was called up as his replacement, Dooley decided to retire from the international scene. He had thus bowed out on a low note – a 17-3 defeat to Ireland in Dublin.

The craggy features of Wade Dooley lit up the England team for eight years and in that time he left his mark on both the game and opponents. He may not always have captured the headlines but his contribution to the cause should never be underestimated. Those who were on the receiving end of some of his crunching challenges may be intrigued to learn that he has recently taken up the altogether more peaceful pursuit of garden design, studying part-time with a view to developing his growing expertise as a possible business interest.

Known as the 'Blackpool Tower', lock forward Wade Dooley was a force to be reckoned with during an impressive domestic and International career

GREAT RUGBY HEROES

WADE DOOLEY

DAVID DUCKHAM

DAVID DUCKHAM

For an English rugby player to earn respect and admiration in Wales, he must be a very special talent indeed. David Duckham, the dashing England wing of the early 1970s, was granted a unique accolade by the Welsh rugby fraternity – he was given his own Welsh nickname, 'Dai'.

What was so different about Duckham that, in Welsh eyes at least, set him apart from other English players of that and previous eras? After all, his record was hardly remarkable – he was on the winning side just eleven times in his 36 internationals. But the Welsh saw him as a player after their own hearts. At a time when England not only played second fiddle to Wales they sometimes weren't even worthy of a place in the orchestra, the Coventry flier stood out from his compatriots. It was like Nureyev joining the Young Generation. The trouble was Duckham hardly ever saw the ball in an England shirt. Left to feed on mere titbits, he only ever got a chance to show what he could do for a few fleeting moments of the 80 minutes. For the rest of the time he either prowled the touchline in frustration or wandered inside in an often fruitless search for a slice of the action. But when he did get the ball and cranked his 6ft 1in, 14-stone frame into gear, he was a joy to watch – a blond blur as he swerved inside and outside on mazy runs towards the opposing line. His sidestep ranked with the best, enabling him to wrong-foot defenders completely. He had flair, he was dynamic, and that was why the Welsh loved him. He was a player in their own image. They thought he was wasted on England. They were probably right.

Duckham started his career as a centre but switched to the wing to take full advantage of his searing pace. He made an instant impact for his country, scoring a try on his debut as England lost 17-15 in Dublin. Then in only his third international he scored both tries in England's 8-3 victory over Scotland at Twickenham. The opportunity to score twice in an England match was to prove a rare luxury for Duckham. Starved of the ball – it has been calculated that during his 36 internationals he received an average of less than three passes per match – his most memorable performances were reserved for other occasions.

Principal among these was the 1971 Lions' tour to New Zealand. As part of a hugely talented back division, Duckham at last received the kind of service his talent merited. He scored eleven tries on the tour, including six against West-Coast/Buller Combined at Greymouth to create a new record for any tourist in New Zealand. Replacing

David Duckham

Born: Coventry, England, 1946

Country: England

Position: Centre, wing

International caps: 36

Clubs: Coventry

Representative honours: British Lions, Barbarians

Welshman John Bevan after the opening game, he played in the last three Tests where, as well as helping out in defence, he launched many a promising attack by operating an incisive scissor movement with full-back J.P.R. Williams.

After helping Coventry to Cup glory in 1972, he once again had the chance to demonstrate his redoubtable powers in the international arena when he was selected to play for the Barbarians against the All Blacks at Twickenham in 1973. In a match that turned out to be arguably the most exciting example ever of free-running rugby, Duckham was in his element. His exemplary handling and sudden changes of direction proved too much for the All Blacks and he crowned a glorious afternoon by side-stepping his way round five New Zealanders before slipping the ball to J.P.R. for the match-clinching try.

After that, it was back to England duty and a regular diet of defeat. His last international, against Scotland at Murrayfield in 1976, ended in a 22-12 loss. That, alas, was pretty much the story of the career of David Duckham, England's only honorary Welshman.

In an international career that spanned seven years, David Duckham won 36 caps but was seldom given the chance to shine

Frik Du Preez

Born: Rustenburg, South Africa, 1935

Country: South Africa

Position: Lock, flanker

International caps: 38

Province/District: Northern Transvaal

GREAT RUGBY HEROES

FRIK DU PREEZ

FRIK DU PREEZ

Frik Du Preez only managed one try in international rugby but it was a score that broke the hearts of the touring British Lions in 1968. Midway through the second half the huge lock gained possession from a lineout some 40 metres from the Lions' line. Instead of transferring the ball infield as expected, Du Preez, in the words of Lions' scrum-half Gareth Edwards, 'came charging round the front of the line like a great big green elephant, gathering speed all the time.' Neither Edwards nor the Lions' wing, Keith Savage, had a prayer of stopping him in full flight. Soon only Irish full-back Tom Kiernan stood between Du Preez and the line. With the South African's mop of jet black hair bouncing wildly, he outwitted Kiernan by means of a beautifully executed shimmy and dived over to score a try that South African fans reckoned was the best seen in the country for at least two decades.

That classic try summed up the remarkable talents of Frederick Christoffel Hendrik Du Preez. He had excellent all-round skills for such a burly man. Although not particularly tall, he was a tower of strength in the lineout, had a fantastic turn of speed and loved nothing more than to run with the ball in one hand while contemptuously fending off would-be challengers with the other. He could sidestep when the mood took him – as it did that day against the Lions – and was a highly accomplished kicker, capable of taking penalties or dropping goals with equal aplomb.

Du Preez made his Springbok debut against England at Twickenham in 1961. He played as a flanker that day (although all bar seven of his Test appearances would be at lock) and his conversion helped the tourists to a 5-0 win. He then followed up with two penalties in his second Test – a 12-5 victory at Murrayfield – and so masterful were the South Africans in terms of international rugby that it was eleven matches and over three years before he tasted defeat. Among the victims during that period were the 1962 British Lions, who lost three and drew one game in four-Test series. Over a period of ten years Du Preez made no fewer than six overseas tours and wore the green and gold shirt in a total of 87 games, coincidentally scoring 87 points. His last Test appearance came at the age of 35 against Australia in 1971 – a rousing 18-6 triumph at Sydney Cricket Ground. His 38 Test matches set a new Springbok record until equalled by loose forward Jan Ellis five years later.

Statistics alone cannot convey the impact he had. At a time when South African rugby was divided by provincial rivalry, the Northern

Transvaal star was popular all the way from Pretoria to Cape Town – home of the Blue Bulls' traditional rivals, Western Province – and at rugby grounds all over the world. His style was uncompromising – even intimidating – but it won him the respect of both colleagues and opponents. Before the Lions' first Test on that 1968 tour, they were warned: 'Watch out for Du Preez. He's something special.' It proved to be sound advice.

A measure of the man's ongoing popularity is that when the Rugby Hall of Fame was introduced in 1997, Du Preez and Danie Craven were the only South Africans to be voted into it. A few years later a poll among the country's fans named the charismatic Du Preez as South Africa's Rugby Player of the Twentieth Century. It was the ultimate accolade, one that brought this comment from Dr Craven, the doyen of South African rugby: 'As long as rugby is played in our country, people who know Frik or knew him, or people who heard of him or read about him, will have a connection with him, and that will enrich our rugby just as Frik did on the playing fields.'

Frik Du Preez's all-round skill made him as ferocious in the tackle as he was skilful on the ball. In his 87 Springboks games, he scored 87 points

JOHN EALES

Australians used to call John Eales 'Nobody' . . . for the simple reason that Nobody's Perfect. With his strength and athleticism he was majestic in the lineout and immensely mobile in the loose while his technical expertise at goalkicking – so unusual for a man of 6ft 7in – brought him 34 penalties and 31 conversions in Test matches alone. But above all he was a superb leader of men, captaining Australia on a record 55 occasions, during which the nation tasted its most successful period ever on the field of rugby. Eales won just about everything worth winning – two World Cups, the Bledisloe Cup, the Tri-Nations tournament and a first-ever series victory against the British Lions. No wonder Wallaby fans could not find fault with the peerless Queenslander.

Eales first appeared in the gold shirt at Ballymore in 1991 as a member of the team that crushed Wales 63-6 and personally won thirteen out of twenty successful Australian lineouts. England were the next opponents where Eales was pitted against 6ft 10in Martin Bayfield. Despite giving away three inches in height, Eales's timing and superb standing jumping completely outgunned Bayfield and powered the Wallabies to a runaway 40-15 win. That year's World Cup started slowly for Australia with Eales twice switching from lock to No. 8 as coach Bob Dwyer changed things around, but a 38-3 victory over Wales in the final pool match (a game in which Eales and Rod McCall won an incredible 28 out of 30 lineouts) set the ball rolling. The final against England was a tense affair, Eales demonstrating another facet to his game with a dramatic try-saving tackle on Rob Andrew in the closing stages. The intervention enabled Australia to scrape home 12-6.

The following year began well for Eales. He scored his first international try against Scotland and then helped Australia to victory over New Zealand in the Bledisloe Cup. Eales was again in superlative form as South Africa were trounced 26-3 in Cape Town but on a tour match in Llanelli he suffered a serious shoulder injury which threatened to end his career. Fortunately he recovered and was fit enough to play in six Tests in 1994. Following a disappointing defeat at the 1995 World Cup, Australia appointed Eales as captain in succession to Michael Lynagh. It was to prove an inspired choice.

With Eales leading by example, Australia became the dominant force in world rugby and in 1999 became the first country to lift the World Cup twice after a 35-12 victory over France at Cardiff's Millennium Stadium. Appropriately, the Wallabies' two most influential

At 6ft 7in, John Eales dominated in the lineout but was also a talented goal kicker, scoring 34 Test penalties and 31 conversions

GREAT RUGBY HEROES

JOHN EALES

players in the tournament, Eales and Tim Horan, had also been members of the triumphant 1991 side.

Ever since 1989 when the nineteen-year-old Eales had watched from the stands at Ballymore as the Lions bulldozed their way to victory, he had longed to lead his country to a first series win against the British tourists. His time came in 2001. The Lions coasted home 29-13 in the first Test but Eales took stock of the situation and the Australians regrouped to take the last two games and the series 2-1. It was one of the proudest moments in Eales's career as he held aloft the Tom Richards Trophy in front of the jubilant Sydney fans. The Tri-Nations tournament was next on the agenda with Australia as defending champions. The outcome rested on the final match in Sydney where, before a capacity crowd of 91,000, Eales's generalship steered the Wallabies to a narrow 29-26 victory over New Zealand. The result was of particular importance to Eales as he had already decided that it would be his last international. Following an emotional farewell speech by Eales himself, Peter Crittle, President of the Australian Rugby Union, stood up and, by way of an address, said simply: 'Thank you, John Eales.' It was a sentiment echoed by the whole of Australia.

John Eales

Born: Brisbane, Australia, 1970

Country: Australia

Position: Lock, No 8

International caps: 86

Clubs: Queensland Reds

Represenattive honours: Queensland

GARETH EDWARDS

GARETH EDWARDS

Even those whose knowledge of Gareth Edwards is confined to that unforgettable try for the Barbarians against the 1973 All Blacks will have observed in that oft-repeated TV clip many of the ingredients that served to make the man from Pontardawe just about the finest rugby player of all time. The upper body strength, the blinding pace, the wonderful athleticism, the awareness and the single-minded determination were there for all to see as he hared down that ever decreasing touchline channel before diving spectacularly over the New Zealand line to score in the corner. It was vintage rugby and vintage Edwards.

An international at nineteen and Wales's youngest captain at twenty, Edwards went on to establish a world record by winning 53 consecutive caps. Over that ten-year period he established formidable half-back partnerships, for both the Lions and Wales, firstly with Barry John and then with Phil Bennett. Blessed with the ability to size up a situation in a split second, he became renowned for his tactical kicking. A master of the low grubber kick that turned the opposition on its heels, he could also relieve pressure on his own forwards by launching hefty punts upfield and even dropped a few goals in his time. A will o' the wisp around the scrum, his handling was impeccable and his finishing deadly, illustrated by his total of 20 Test tries.

Like many boys raised in Welsh mining valleys, Edwards always dreamed of scoring the winning try against England. The difference was that he was able to live the dream. As a pupil at Pontardawe Technical School, his fledgling talents were recognised by his games master, Bill Samuel, who encouraged him to play at scrum-half and concentrated on developing his attributes for that specialist position. After winning caps for Welsh Secondary Schools, he was called up for his international debut against France on April Fool's Day 1967 and by the following February was leading out the team against Scotland. Having impressed on a tour to South Africa with his club, Cardiff, Edwards returned to that country with the 1968 Lions and emerged as one of the few successes until his participation was curtailed by a hamstring injury. Previously criticised for slow passing, he greatly improved his distribution by perfecting the spin-pass, a trick he had borrowed from the All Black Chris Laidlaw.

With the inventive, quicksilver Edwards at scrum-half, Wales came to be the dominant force in rugby through the 1970s. Alongside him Barry

Gareth Edwards

Born: Pontardawe, Wales, 1947

Country: Wales

Position: Scrum-half

International caps: 53

Clubs: Cardiff, Cardiff College of Education

Representative honours: British Lions, Barbarians

John revelled in the opportunities presented by his partner's fast, accurate service. They played 23 Tests together over the next four years, their partnership reaching its peak on the 1971 Lions' tour of New Zealand. If John was the All Blacks' executioner, it was Edwards who sharpened the blade.

When John retired, Edwards took over his role as tactical maestro. He went on a third Lions' tour – to South Africa in 1974 – and, relishing the bone-hard pitches, played a major part in the comprehensive 3-0 series win. His absence from the 1977 tour to New Zealand was cited by many as the reason for the Lions' defeat. That was how important he was to British rugby.

Of course, nowhere did they appreciate that more than in Wales. During Edwards' reign Wales won three Grand Slams, five Triple Crowns, five outright Championships and two shared titles. He retired after the completion of that third Grand Slam, his last international being a 16-7 victory over France in front of his adoring Cardiff fans. He later became a team captain on television's *A Question of Sport*.

There will always be a special place in Welsh hearts for the boy who started off playing rugby in the streets of Pontardawe and ended up gracing the finest stadia in the world.

With Ireland's Willie John McBride bearing down on him, Gareth Edwards delivers a classic scrum-half dive pass

MARK ELLA

MARK ELLA

An outstanding try scorer and tactician, Mark Ella's international career was cut tragically short by injury

That Mark Ella has gone down in history as one of the world's greatest-ever fly-halves despite retiring prematurely at the age of 25 is testimony to the immense talent he displayed in his all-too-short career. Rarely has Australia seen such a wonderfully gifted athlete who could run, pass and kick with equal aplomb. He had natural ability by the bucketload, an outstanding individual entertainer who was also able to harness his skills within the framework of the team.

Mark was one of three Aboriginal brothers to play for the Wallabies. Mark, his twin Glen and younger brother Gary developed their rugby skills in the unlikely setting of the backyard of their Sydney home. For hours on end the boys practised looping movements whereby Mark, having made a pass, would keep running around the outside to take the return ball. The brothers' dedication paid off when they were selected for the Australian Schools' party that visited Britain during 1977-78. One of the highlights of the tour was a comprehensive defeat of the Welsh Secondary Schools XV at Cardiff Arms Park. Mark, in particular, caught the eye, prompting seasoned observers to jot down his name as one to watch for the future.

By then the boys had been spotted by Bob Dwyer, coach of Sydney's Randwick club, and were such a sensation at under-15 level that, at the age of just seventeen, they were promoted to the first grade where they were nicknamed 'The Invincibles'. By means of their highly individual loop technique, they proceeded to transform back play at the club. As fly-half, Mark would stand unusually close to the scrum-half, thereby pulling opposition back row forwards towards him at an angle that made it difficult for them to change direction and harass the Randwick midfield. Once in possession of the ball, Mark would move it on quickly to the centres, often continuing his run on an extended loop so that he would appear again in the line either between centre and wing or sometimes even outside his wing. He was not one for standing back and admiring a move he had started; he wanted to be involved in every phase until it had reached a successful conclusion. This flat back line proved so profitable for Randwick that it was subsequently adopted by the national team once Mark had been selected for his Wallaby debut, against New Zealand in June 1980.

Although Glen and Gary each played in four Tests, Mark was clearly the outstanding member of the trio and in 1982 was given the honour of captaining his country. Ironically it was Mark's uncharacteristic error that allowed his boyhood hero, Graham Mourie, to score a crucial try in the first Test that helped New Zealand win the Bledisloe Cup series 2-1. However during that rubber Mark linked up with David Campese for the first time to forge an understanding that would bear fruit two years later. By then Mark had lost the captaincy to Queensland's solid, reliable Andrew Slack but he answered any critics in the best possible way with a series of breathtaking displays on the Wallabies' 1984 tour to the British Isles. The Australians were in unstoppable form, winning all four Tests, and Mark Ella scored a try in each – a repeat of his achievement on that 1977-78 tour with Australian Schoolboys. His sensational try in the 37-12 win at Murrayfield brought the house down. Yet it would be his last international.

For just as Australian fans were licking their lips at the prospect of seeing Mark Ella in a gold jersey for many years to come, he stunned the rugby world by announcing his retirement, citing a mysterious neck injury. If he had played on, he would surely have written his name into many pages of the record books. As it is, we are left with only fleeting glimpses of what might have been.

Mark Ella

Born: Sydney, Australia, 1959

Country: Australia

Position: Fly-half

International caps: 25

Clubs: Randwick

Representative honours: New South Wales

NICK FARR-JONES

When Nick Farr-Jones was named captain of Australia in 1988, the reaction to his appointment was decidedly mixed. His predecessor, Andrew Slack, had been sacked in the wake of Australia's disappointing showing at the 1987 World Cup and whilst it was generally accepted that Farr-Jones was the best scrum-half in the world at the time, there were those who accused him of not having the mental toughness to handle the pressures of leading his country. But the Sydney lawyer was to put forward a compelling case for the defence, turning the side's fortunes around and leading them to a World Cup triumph in 1991, as a result of which he was hailed instead as one of Australia's all-time great captains.

Born in Carringbah, New South Wales, Farr-Jones showed as a teenager that he had all the makings of a top-class scrum-half. Although tall for a player operating in that position, he was exceptionally strong – an attribute that enabled him to work in attack and defence like an extra back-row forward. But what particularly made him stand out at that age was his cool decision-making, convincing

Nick Farr-Jones overcame his detractors to captain Australia 36 times and become part of a 'Holy Trinity' with Michael Lynagh and David Campese

some observers that he was future captaincy material.

He continued to progress while playing for Sydney University (where he was studying law) and in 1984 was called up for the Wallabies' tour of Britain and Ireland. That Australian team was a formidable unit, completing the Grand Slam of home nations, and the intelligent, nimble Farr-Jones played his part. He made his international debut in the 19-3 victory over England at Twickenham and kept his place for the remaining three Tests. He showed tremendous confidence for a 22-year-old, taking a lot of the pressure off Mark Ella and even weighing in with a try in the final Test against Scotland. Although he was again in sparkling form when New Zealand were defeated two years later, the inaugural World Cup left a cloud over Australian rugby. When Farr-Jones was controversially made captain, early results did little to dissuade the doubters. Humiliated in the Bledisloe Cup, the Wallabies endured a torrid tour of the UK and then in 1989, as the Lions won a hard-fought series 2-1, Farr-Jones was taught a few lessons by opposite number Robert Jones, prompting further mutterings about his temperament. And when the All Blacks romped into a 2-0 lead in the 1990 Bledisloe Cup, the knives were out for Farr-Jones and coach Bob Dwyer.

The turnaround in fortunes began when Farr-Jones and Dwyer restructured the battered and bruised Australian pack. Their work paid dividends with a shock 21-9 victory in the third Test after Farr-Jones had instructed his men to face out the All Blacks at the haka. Farr-Jones and centre Tim Horan celebrated the result by swimming naked in the icy waters of Wellington harbour! Just as that performance gave the Australians confidence, it unsettled New Zealand who succumbed to another defeat – 21-12 in Sydney – a year later. Although the All Blacks won the return match in Auckland 6-3, they had no answer when the two nations met in the crunch game – the semi-final of the 1991 World Cup. Australia won 16-6 and went on to beat England in the final. Farr-Jones was now lauded as part of a 'Holy Trinity' with Michael Lynagh and Campese. Indeed the scrum-half's contribution to Campese's success should not be under-estimated. It is said that of Campese's 64 Test tries, Farr-Jones played a hand in at least 46.

After leading his side to victory in the 1992 Bledisloe Cup and in a one-off Test in Cape Town, Farr-Jones retired from the international game, but was persuaded back for one last series against South Africa the following year. Although no longer skipper, he inspired the Wallabies to a 2-1 series win before retiring for good, having captained his country 36 times and scored nine tries. The doubters had been made to eat their words.

GREAT RUGBY HEROES

NICK FARR-JONES

Nick Farr-Jones

Born: Carringbah, Australia, 1962

Country: Australia

Position: Scrum-half

International caps: 63

Clubs: Sydney University

Representative honours: New South Wales

SEAN FITZPATRICK

SEAN FITZPATRICK

The most capped New Zealander in history, Sean Fitzpatrick owed his achievement not only to his incredible fitness and staying power but also to a few slices of luck along the way.

The son of Brian Fitzpatrick, who played 22 times for his country between 1951 and 1954, Sean was educated at Sacred Heart College in Auckland and played for New Zealand Secondary Schools in 1981. He made his debut as hooker for Auckland three years later but was unable to hold down a regular place because his throwing into lineouts was apparently considered too wayward.

Then in 1986 came the first of his fortuitous breaks. Most of the established All Blacks had been suspended for going on the rebel tour to South Africa and Fitzpatrick, although not yet first choice with Auckland, was selected as reserve hooker for the Test against France at Christchurch. And when Bruce Hemara had to withdraw because of injury, Fitzpatrick suddenly found himself propelled into the starting line-up, helping New Zealand to an 18-9 win. With the rebels still ineligible, he kept his place against Australia but lost it for the remaining domestic Tests. However, he forced his way back into the side at the end of the year in France, beginning an unbroken sequence of 63 Tests, spanning nine years.

Here again Fitzpatrick was indebted to Dame Fortune. He was only expecting to attend the 1987 World Cup as understudy to New Zealand captain Andy Dalton but when Dalton was injured, Fitzpatrick went on to play in every match.

Third time lucky came in 1992 when the selectors were deliberating who to choose as the next New Zealand captain. Coach Laurie Mains had made no secret that his preference was for Mike Brewer but when Brewer was injured in a trial match, his enforced absence opened the door for Fitzpatrick. Of course it is one thing to be fortunate and another to take full advantage of the situation, but Fitzpatrick seized the opportunity with both hands. Pretenders to the throne were swatted aside by his supreme fitness levels and unyielding will to win. Second best was not in Fitzpatrick's vocabulary and when his standards briefly slipped during the defeat to the British Lions in the second Test at Wellington in 1993, he was so taken aback by the vociferous nature of the criticism hurled at him that coach Mains felt compelled to speak out on his behalf. The same ground provided happier memories for Fitzpatrick three years later when New Zealand crucified Australia 43-6 with a performance that has rarely been bettered in the history of rugby.

Sean Fitzpatrick

Born: Auckland, New Zealand, 1963

Country: New Zealand

Position: Hooker

International caps: 92

Clubs: Auckland University

Representative honours: Auckland, Southern Hemisphere

Victory in the 1996 Tri-Nations series against Australia and South Africa was surpassed the following month as Fitzpatrick led his team into battle against the Springboks, aiming to be the first New Zealand captain to win a Test series in South Africa. His men responded magnificently, the All Blacks taking the series 2-1 and giving Fitzpatrick further cause to write his name in the record books. New national coach John Hart, the man who had been in charge of Auckland when the youngster couldn't get into the provincial team, expressed the hope that Fitzpatrick would still be around for the 1999 World Cup but any chances of doing so or of reaching 100 Test caps were dashed by an injury to his right knee that led him to miss much of the second half of 1997. He fought on through a miserable tour of Britain and Ireland before announcing his retirement in April 1998. He had captained his country on a record 51 occasions.

Fitzpatrick's dedication was second to none while his mobility and strength enabled him to shape the prototype of the modern hooker. And by the time he retired he was considered to be one of the best lineout throwers in the world. He had come a long way – thanks to the occasional helping hand.

Lucky breaks let Sean Fitzpatrick make the All Black No. 2 jersey his own but his talent and dedication were what made him the most-capped All Black ever

GRANT FOX

Despite his phenomenal reputation as a goal kicker, Grant Fox was twice left out of the All Black line-up at the peak of his ability

GRANT FOX

Until Andrew Mehrtens came along, Grant Fox was the most prolific points scorer that New Zealand rugby had ever seen – a goalkicking machine who sent records tumbling at every level he played. Perhaps his most remarkable achievement was that he passed Don Clarke's New Zealand record of 207 points in Test matches in only his second season as a regular choice.

Yet there was so much more to Fox's game than kicking goals. A shrewd player with an astute tactical brain, he was a great thinker who used his awareness of what was going on around him to organise the entire New Zealand backline. His ability to plan and execute strategies in the heat of battle won as many games as his kicking.

After captaining the New Zealand Secondary Schools side that toured Australia in 1980, Fox made his debut for Auckland in 1982 and first represented his country in two matches on a tour of Fiji in October 1984. However it would be another three years before he established himself as New Zealand's regular goalkicker. Having been selected for the abandoned tour of South Africa in 1985, he made his first Test appearance on the replacement trip to Argentina but was dropped for the second Test. The following year he went on the unauthorised tour to South Africa, eventually regaining his All Black place on the visit to France although he was not picked for either of the Tests. Then in 1987 his luck changed. He played in the opening match of the inaugural World Cup – a 70-6 rout of Italy – and never looked back. Fox's total of 126 points in that year's tournament remains a World Cup record and firmly established him as one of the leading lights of New Zealand rugby. So many of the team's most incisive moves revolved around him and he was a central figure in their run of 23 Tests without defeat between 1987 and 1990. And it was on the 1988 tour of Australia that he blew away Don Clarke's 24-year-old record.

He created another landmark the following year by scoring 433 points in first-class rugby in the course of the New Zealand domestic season.

His only Test try came against Scotland in 1990 and he kicked off the following year's World Cup by scoring 14 points in the 18-12 win over England. Further victories over the USA, Italy and Canada swept the All Blacks to the semi-final but, despite Fox's 44 points for the tournament, he was powerless to prevent Australia winning 16-6. In the same year he played for a Southern Hemisphere team that beat the Northern Hemisphere 39-4 in Hong Kong.

Grant Fox

Born: New Plymouth, New Zealand, 1962

Country: New Zealand

Position: Fly-half

International caps: 46

Clubs: Auckland University

Representative honours: Auckland

Remarkably, in view of Fox's kicking expertise, whether for goal or position, two of New Zealand's coaches thought they could do without his services. John Hart had dropped him for the tour of Japan in 1987 and now Laurie Mains deemed Fox surplus to requirements for the 1992 centenary series. Both men quickly realised the error of their ways. It was impossible to replace the irreplaceable.

Restored to favour, Fox destroyed the British Lions in 1993. His dramatic last-minute kick in the first Test at Christchurch gave New Zealand a slender 20-18 victory and he finished the three-match rubber with 32 points – over half of his side's total. After that triumphant Test series, he played only two more Tests – against Australia at Dunedin and Samoa at Auckland – before deciding to retire.

He finished with 645 points in Test matches (currently second only to Mehrtens in the New Zealand list) and kicked 128 penalties and 118 conversions. In all matches for the All Blacks he amassed an incredible 1,067 points from just 78 games. He was, by anyone's standards, a prodigious talent.

DANIE GERBER

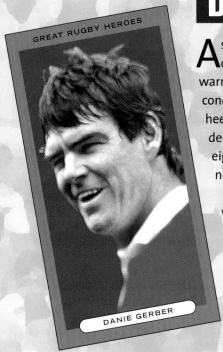

GREAT RUGBY HEROES

DANIE GERBER

As England found to their cost in 1984, Danie Gerber was the master of opportunism. The dynamic Springbok centre had sounded a warning with a try in the first Test at Port Elizabeth that helped condemn England to a 33-15 defeat. However, the warning was not heeded and in the second Test at Ellis Park, Johannesburg, he destroyed the tourists with a sensational hat-trick of tries in just eighteen minutes, South Africa going on to win 35-9. England would not forget the name of Danie Gerber in a hurry.

Indeed had it not been for the political situation in South Africa, which restricted the country's sporting contact with other nations throughout Gerber's twelve-year international career (the Springboks didn't take part in either of the first two World Cups), he would surely have achieved superstar status, right up there with the likes of Campese and Lomu. Certainly he had all the attributes, as is proved by his record of nineteen tries in only 24 Tests. At 6ft tall and weighing nearly fourteen stone, he was the ideal build for a centre. He was a fitness fanatic whose job as a sports administrator allowed him to begin each day with a two-hour training schedule, starting with a rapid 300 sit-ups. This regime developed his speed and strength, making him fierce in the tackle and incredibly quick off the mark. What's more he built up the stamina to maintain that speed over distances of 40 metres or more, his powerful thighs more often than not driving him to the line ahead of covering defenders. South Africa's *Sunday Times* wrote of Gerber: 'With his balance, speed and power, he could turn a centimetre into a metre. And when he broke the line, it was invariably a try. Every time this explosive player got the ball, there was a sense of anticipation.'

Gerber first created an impression as a Junior Springbok against Bill Beaumont's 1980 Lions, making his full international debut later in the year on the two-Test tour of South America and scoring a try in both games. The home countries experienced their first taste of this exciting new talent when Ireland embarked on a short tour of South Africa in 1981. Gerber ran in two tries in the first Test at Cape Town as Ireland were beaten 23-15. In the first part of his Test career he formed a formidable midfield partnership with Willie du Plessis, the pair appearing together in eight Tests. Later Gerber would team up in six Tests with Willie's younger brother, Michael.

There were further tours of South America in 1982 and 1984, both of which showed Gerber to be at the peak of his form. He scored four tries

Danie Gerber

Born: Port Elizabeth, South Africa, 1958

Country: South Africa

Position: Centre

International caps: 24

Clubs: L'Aquila

Representative honours: Eastern Province, Western Province, Barbarians in the two-Test series of 1982 (including a hat-trick in the first Test) and followed up with two more in the 1984 series. With the aforementioned demolition of England sandwiched in between, it meant that he scored ten tries in just six Tests over that two-year period – a phenomenal achievement. Meanwhile he was able to reach a wider audience by turning out for the Barbarians, scoring twice to commemorate the opening of Murrayfield's new stand and going over four times against Cardiff. One try, which had begun deep inside the Barbarians' 22, ranked alongside the best ever seen at the Arms Park.

In 1986 the rebel New Zealand Cavaliers toured South Africa on an unofficial tour. With the rubber tied at 1-1, the visitors nurtured hopes of a first series win in South Africa until Gerber sprinted 35 metres for a wonderful try that broke the tourists' resistance. New Zealand ended up on the wrong end of a 33-18 scoreline and then lost the final Test by fourteen points.

He eventually retired after a defeat at Twickenham in 1992 and is now assistant coach to South African team the Pumas. If ever there was a player whose talent deserved to be seen on a wider stage, it was Danie Gerber.

Danie Gerber clashes with Rob Andrew at Twickenham in his final game for the Springboks

GREAT RUGBY HEROES

MIKE GIBSON

MIKE GIBSON

Mike Gibson did not look or behave like a stereotypical rugby player. Quiet, thoughtful and teetotal, he possessed a build that suggested he was more likely to get sand kicked in his face than inflict crunching tackles on the world's most fearsome forwards. Yet what Gibson perhaps lacked in physique, he more than made up for in courage and determination. And it was these qualities – combined with no small measure of skill – that won him a reputation as the most consistent British player over a fifteen-year period and earned him a record number of Test caps for Ireland.

Some even considered him to be the best all-round back in the world at his peak – no mean feat when one realises that among his contemporaries was a certain Barry John.

There were few more conscientious trainers than the Belfast solicitor. He prepared thoroughly for each game, both mentally and physically, the results being there for all to see on the pitch. In

possession he demonstrated immaculate judgement, knowing precisely when to release the ball to the man on the outside, and when tackling and covering he displayed admirable tenacity. Furthermore, even in the twilight of his career he never lost that assured handling or the ability to be the first to spot a gap and when he made his final international appearance, against Australia in June 1979, he became at 36 years and 195 days, the oldest Irishman to win a Test cap.

Gibson prepared for his international career first as a player with Campbell College, Belfast, and then with Cambridge University. He graduated to the international ranks in 1964, playing at fly-half in Ireland's 18-5 win at Twickenham, their first success on that ground for sixteen years. For the 1966 Lions' tour to New Zealand he switched to centre to accommodate the mercurial Welshman David Watkins. Playing in all four Tests, Gibson was one of the few to emerge with any credit as the Lions suffered a whitewash.

His versatility made him an invaluable member of any touring party. In 1968 in South Africa he returned to playing at fly-half in the Tests after Barry John had fractured his collar-bone during the opening international at Ellis Park. Coming on for John in that match, Gibson became the first British player to win a cap as a replacement. A marked man, Gibson found himself on the receiving end of some rough treatment from the Springboks but played to his usual high standard although the series ended in a dismal 3-0 defeat for the Lions with one Test drawn.

The 1971 tour to New Zealand saw Gibson – and the Lions – at their best. This time Gibson was playing at centre, alongside John, and they complemented each other splendidly, Gibson again demonstrating his ability to adapt to the playing styles of different partners. The New Zealanders were repeatedly put on the back foot by Gibson's rapier-like thrusts and when they ventured on to the attack, they were often frustrated by his sense of anticipation. He went on tour twice more with the Lions – in 1974 and 1977, thereby equalling fellow countryman Willie John McBride's record of five Lions' tours — but did not feature in Tests on those later occasions. When he finally called it a day, Gibson held the world record of 81 international appearances to his name – 69 for Ireland and twelve for the Lions.

There have been more glamorous, more flamboyant, players in the history of British rugby than Mike Gibson, but few who could compete with his consistency and durability over such a long period. Both for the Lions and Ireland, whom he helped to a shared Five Nations title in 1973 and outright victory the following year, the Ulsterman revealed that beneath that polished veneer lay a steely competitive streak.

Irish fly-half Mike Gibson was to equal fellow Irishman Willie John McBride's record of five British Lions' tours

Mike Gibson

Born: Belfast, Northern Ireland, 1942

Country: Ireland

Position: Fly-half, centre

International caps: 69

Clubs: Cambridge University, North of Ireland

Representative honours: British Lions, Barbarians

JEREMY GUSCOTT

Former bricklayer Jeremy Guscott celebrated his first appearance for England against Romania in 1989 with a hat trick of tries

Jeremy Guscott

Born: Bath, England, 1965

Country: England

Position: Centre

International caps: 65

Clubs: Bath

Representative honours: British Lions, Barbarians

JEREMY GUSCOTT

When Jeremy Guscott announced his retirement in 1999 after ten years at the top, England coach Clive Woodward enthused: 'Jerry Guscott has been an invaluable support to younger players and an England centre to remember. He epitomised the best in English rugby.'

Indeed he did. His total of 30 Test tries puts him second in England's all-time list behind Rory Underwood but he provided much more than mere points to the national team. For Guscott gave an often dour side a much-needed element of glamour, his silky smooth running from behind the scrum coming as a welcome relief to the relentless push and shove of England's forward-dominated game. He formed a world record centre pairing of 43 Tests with Will Carling who provided the muscle while Guscott supplied the pace and tries. Guscott's electrifying speed made him the one England back consistently capable of unlocking a tight defence although his talents were under-employed in all too many matches. But when he was given a chance to shine, he was poetry in motion.

An interesting mix of nonchalance and arrogance, Guscott first burst onto the scene in 1989. He began playing mini-rugby with his local club, Bath, as a seven-year-old and managed to overcome early problems, including being expelled from school, to fulfil his extraordinary talent. Unlike most of his England team-mates, he did not boast a public school, university-educated background and in his early days as an international, when the game was still amateur, he paid his way in life by working as a bricklayer and later as a public relations man for British Gas. As his fame spread, he was able to capitalise on his cool, laid-back image by doing modelling work.

He marked his international debut against Romania with a hat-trick of tries, as a result of which he was chosen for that summer's tour of Australia by the Lions. Omitted from the first Test, which ended in a crushing defeat, he was promptly called up for the second international at Brisbane and clinched victory five minutes from the finish with a wonderful solo try. This made him the first man since Jeff Butterfield in 1955 to score on his debuts for both England and the Lions.

Adding strong defensive tackling to his running game, Guscott played a major part in England's back-to-back Grand Slams of 1991 and 1992, along with their progress to the final of the World Cup. A serious groin injury hampered his progress in 1993-94 but he bounced back to help England to another Grand Slam in 1995. However, arguably his greatest achievement came on the Lions' tour of South Africa in 1997.

Having been written off in advance by the South African media and public, the Lions put on a storming show to win the first Test in Cape Town by nine points. The second Test at Durban was all square at 15-15 entering the final moments when Guscott landed a glorious drop goal to win the match and the series.

Away from the international arena, Guscott enjoyed tremendous success with Bath, helping the club to become the dominant force in English rugby in the early 1990s with a string of League titles and Pilkington Cup triumphs. He finished with a total of 67 first-class tries and 333 points (143 of them in England Tests).

Since retirement, Guscott's profile has been almost as high as that of his old team-mate Will Carling. After being acquitted of assaulting a pedestrian who had allegedly stepped out in front of his car, he has enjoyed a lucrative television career, first as a presenter of *Gladiators* and currently as a BBC rugby analyst. He was awarded the MBE in 2000 for services to rugby.

GAVIN HASTINGS

Gavin Hastings could hardly have made a worse start to his international career. Kicking off against France at Murrayfield in 1986, he succeeded in putting the ball out on the full whereupon the French ran back at their bewildered opponents to score a try without a single Scottish player touching the ball. Things could only get better. And they did.

Gavin Hastings was not one to dwell on a moment of misfortune, a jangling of nerves. Instead he showed true grit by kicking a Scottish record six penalties in that match to lift his team to a dramatic and unlikely 18-17 victory. The Scots had a new Braveheart.

The Edinburgh-born full-back would eventually captain his country on 20 occasions – second only to David Sole. A quiet but inspirational leader, he used his presence and inner strength to motivate those around him. He wasn't one for impassioned pre-match speeches but instead preferred to coax and cajole his players into giving 110 per cent. He was never better than when his back was against the wall – a position with which he became all too familiar during his later years with Scotland – and from where he could instigate a determined fightback. An outstanding goalkicker, his total of 140 Test penalties is more than double that of his nearest Scottish rival, Andy Irvine, and his 86 conversions in Tests is also an emphatic Scottish record. In open play he used his imposing 6ft 2in, fifteen-stone frame to burst into the line at opportune moments, scoring seventeen tries in Test matches. In all he compiled a record 667 Test points for Scotland and his combined total of 733 for Scotland and the Lions set a new British points-scoring standard.

One of four brothers, three of whom played for the Scottish Schools while at George Watson's School in Edinburgh, Gavin captained Cambridge University before making his international debut in the same match as younger brother Scott, a barnstorming centre who would go on to win 65 caps – four more than his illustrious sibling. Thereafter Gavin carried on from where he had left off against France, employing that mighty boot to kick eight conversions in two 1987 World Cup matches – against Zimbabwe and Romania. Two years later he was selected as first choice full-back on the Lions' triumphant tour of Australia and cemented his standing as a true world-class player. He had already given notice of his intentions in the match with New South Wales where he seized upon a loose kick by David Campese and dummied his way through for a try that helped the Lions to a 23-21 victory. After the Lions lost the first Test in Sydney, it was Gavin who, taking a pass from brother Scott, went over for the try that turned the second match in their favour. He then kicked five penalties in the final Test to see the Lions home 19-18, bringing his tour total to 66 points.

Fresh from his success, Hastings guaranteed himself a place in Scottish folklore by playing a major role in the country's 1990 Grand Slam – only their third ever. The following year he helped them to the semi-finals of the World Cup and then in 1993 captained the Lions to New Zealand where, despite fielding an ageing pack, they put on a gutsy show before going down 2-1. Elevated to captain of his country, he marked the 1995 Championship by guiding Scotland to their first-ever win at the Parc des Princes, leading from the front by scoring the winning try himself. His swansong was captaining Scotland at that year's World Cup. Proving that age had not diminished his powers, he notched a record 44 points (including nine conversions) in the 89-0 rout of the Ivory Coast. His last game in Scotland colours was the quarter-final defeat to New Zealand where, incidentally, they considered Gavin Hastings to be the finest full-back in the world.

Asked once for his verdict on Jonah Lomu, Hastings replied: 'There's no doubt about it – he's a big bastard.' That was Gavin Hastings: always understated.

GREAT RUGBY HEROES

GAVIN HASTINGS

All-time Scottish record holder for kicking penalties and conversions, full-back Gavin Hastings was never happier than when he was running with the ball in his hands

Gavin Hastings

Born: Edinburgh, Scotland, 1962

Country: Scotland

Position: Full-back

International caps: 61

Clubs: Cambridge University, London Scottish, Watsonians

Representative honours: British Lions, Barbarians

ANDY IRVINE

Only the legendary J.P.R. Williams could deny Scotland's Andy Irvine the British Lions' full-back jersey

Andy Irvine

Born: Edinburgh, Scotland, 1951

Country: Scotland

Position: Full-back

International caps: 51

Clubs: Heriot's Former Pupils

Representative honours: British Lions, Barbarians

ANDY IRVINE

Over a period of ten years at international level Andy Irvine developed into one of the first true stars of rugby north of the border. It was a career that earned him what was, at the time, a record number of Scottish caps yet one that would surely have brought much greater reward but for the fact that he was usually part of a pretty ordinary Scotland team. There was also one other obstacle barring Irvine's path to world recognition – J.P.R. Williams.

When the International Board changed the Law relating to kicking direct to touch in 1968, a new breed of full-back was created to take advantage of the fresh attacking possibilities. Irvine was one such player, so was the Welsh doctor. Unfortunately for Irvine he was destined to spend much of the early part of his international career in the shadow of Williams who was rightly seen as the foremost full-back in British – and indeed world – rugby. However, Irvine was nothing if not adaptable and played on the wing for the 1974 Lions before eventually securing the full-back spot as his own when Williams declined to tour New Zealand three years later.

Irvine in full flight was a sight to behold. Blessed with tremendous pace for such a big man, he would charge through the opposing ranks like a rampaging bull. An exciting free runner, he was the scorer of spectacular tries from either wing or full-back and was also a redoubtable goalkicker, able to land penalties from distances of up to 60 metres. His total of 61 penalties in Tests for Scotland is second only to that of Gavin Hastings. Irvine's Achilles' heel was his inability to deal with a high ball under pressure. The opposition would play on this, launching garryowens into the sky and hoping to capitalise on Irvine's obvious discomfort. It was this defensive frailty that put him behind the safe and solid J.P.R. in the pecking order.

Irvine followed in the footsteps of Dan Drysdale and Ken Scotland as former pupils of the George Heriot School in Edinburgh who went on to play full-back for Scotland. First capped against the All Blacks in 1972, he made his name when touring South Africa with the 1974 Lions. Although second choice full-back to J.P.R., he was selected at wing-threequarter for the last two Tests as a replacement for Billy Steele and responded with two penalties and a conversion in the third Test at Port Elizabeth and a penalty and a try in the final drawn match in Johannesburg. He finished with 156 points on the tour, establishing a record for a Lion in South Africa.

He toured again in 1977 and this time, in the absence of J.P.R., as full-back. He thrilled the New Zealand crowds with his powerful running, scoring five tries against King Country/Wanganui Combined (a record for a Lions full-back) and a magnificent solo try against the Hanan Shield Districts in which he beat player after player in a mazy run, littered with swerves and jinks, before touching down. He went on to score 25 points in that match, equalling Malcolm Thomas's 1959 points-scoring record for a Lion in New Zealand.

When J.P.R. announced his first retirement in 1979, Irvine formally assumed the mantle of number one full-back. In 1980 he went to South Africa on his third Lions' tour and in the same year was appointed captain of Scotland. He led his country in 15 Tests before retiring in 1982 with what was then a Scottish record of 273 points in Test matches. Not that Andy Irvine would have boasted about it. He wasn't that sort of man. Quietly spoken and unassuming, he just loved to play rugby in whatever position was available. And he did so with some style.

DICKIE JEEPS

Dickie Jeeps had the relatively rare distinction of playing for the British Lions before he ever played for his country

Richard Eric Gautrey Jeeps, known to all as 'Dickie', was English rugby's most familiar face in the 1950s. An impish, tenacious scrum-half, he had the distinction of being selected for the British Lions before he was capped for England. He eventually made up for lost time by playing a key role in England's 1957 Grand Slam and going on to captain his country thirteen times.

In his heyday, Jeeps was considered the best scrum-half in the world. Aside from his quick hands and feet, he was one of the game's great thinkers, always ready to come up with new ploys to unsettle the opposition. He possessed great tactical appreciation but preferred to cut through the jargon, once remarking: 'There is far too much talk about good ball and bad ball. In my opinion, good ball is when you have possession and bad ball is when the opposition have it.'

But it was his courage that set him apart. Utterly fearless, he preferred to accept all manner of physical punishment rather than pass on bad ball to his fly-half and was prepared to take a battering in order to prevent the opposition locks driving through the lineout. Nowhere was this selfless attitude better illustrated than on the Lions' tour to New Zealand in 1959 where he was an indomitable presence in attack and defence. The home crowds warmed to the little man as he repeatedly bounced back from everything the huge All Black forwards could throw at him until a hip injury sustained in a savage third Test at Christchurch brought a premature end to his tour. At the end of that same match he paraded an array of bruises that stretched half-way down one side of his body.

GREAT RUGBY HEROES

DICKIE JEEPS

The product of Cambridgeshire farming stock, Jeeps played for the local city club before moving on to Northampton where his outstanding form led to calls for him to be included in the national set-up. While the England selectors dithered, the Lions took the uncapped 23-year-old as a third scrum-half on the tour of South Africa to counter the high risk of injury in that position. It was assumed that it would require misfortune to befall his two rivals for Jeeps to have any chance of playing in the Tests but in the provincial warm-up matches he began to develop a fine understanding with fly-half Cliff Morgan who thrived on Jeeps' fast, accurate passes. Consequently, the pair teamed up in the first Test at Johannesburg where Jeeps expertly supplied the pass for Morgan's try that helped the Lions home 23-22.

The series was drawn 2-2 but Jeeps' gritty performances stirred the England selectors into action and he finally won his first cap, against Wales in 1956. His irrepressible spirit inspired both his country and the Lions over the next six years and such was his mental and physical toughness that on his remaining two Lions' tours a third scrum-half was deemed superfluous. A year after that battling trip to New Zealand he was named England captain. His first result in charge was a 14-6 victory over Wales at Twickenham and he proceeded to steer the team to a share of the Five Nations title with France.

The 1962 season was his last. After making a final England appearance against Scotland, he was one of the mainstays of an indifferent Lions' side in South Africa, finishing with thirteen Test appearances for the Lions, a total bettered only by Willie John McBride. To mark his outstanding service, Jeeps was made captain for the concluding game of the Lions' tour.

He may have finished playing but there was no keeping the ebullient Jeeps out of the spotlight for long. He became an outspoken chairman of the Sports Council, an England selector and President of the Rugby Football Union, carrying out these duties with the same energy and resilience that characterised his playing days.

Dickie Jeeps

Born: Chesterton, England, 1931

Country: England

Position: Scrum-half

International caps: 24

Clubs: Cambridge, Northampton

Representative honours: British Lions, Barbarians

BARRY JOHN

BARRY JOHN

New Zealand rugby fans are not renowned for their generosity towards opposing players. So when they christened Barry John 'The King' in honour of his performances for the touring Lions of 1971, you knew that it was no hollow praise but an acknowledgement that they had been in the presence of a very special talent. In six short years as an international, John became a sporting superstar, his profile enhanced by improved television coverage of the game. In terms of status and ability, he was the George Best of rugby, but that was where the similarity ended for the grounded John was more likely to be seen in a workingmen's club than Stringfellow's.

So why was Barry John such a revered figure? The basic statistics (25 Welsh caps yielding five tries and 90 points) are scarcely remarkable but figures alone cannot paint the full picture of the gifted young athlete who tamed the mighty All Blacks and fired his country to a Grand Slam, a Triple Crown, and a shared Championship. He formed a deadly partnership with Gareth Edwards that unlocked the best defences in the world, exploiting the spaces with the pin-point accuracy of his kicking. He landed penalties with an innovative round-the-corner style, seemed able to drop goals at will and was a silky smooth runner, gliding and swerving through previously invisible gaps in the opposition ranks. And like all great sportsmen, he appeared to do everything effortlessly, in his own time. Barry John was never hurried or harassed.

The slim youth from Cefneithin learned his art from watching Carwyn James play for Llanelli and made his international debut against Australia at Cardiff in 1966, ousting David Watkins. It was no fairytale start, Australia winning 14-11, and John was soon dropped. It was not until the autumn of 1967, by which time Watkins had turned professional, that John was given a prolonged run in tandem with his Cardiff team-mated Edwards. Despite having only once been on the winning side in an international, John was chosen for the 1968 Lions' tour to South Africa but fractured his collar-bone in the first Test. After guiding Wales to a Triple Crown in 1969, he joined the national side on a tour to New Zealand, which, although not a success in terms of results, considerably furthered his education.

He returned to Wales a better player, ready to enter the years from 1970 to 1972 when he was at the peak of his powers. A shared title with France in 1970 was followed by the 1971 Grand Slam – Wales's first for nineteen years – and then that triumphant Lions' tour of New

Barry John

Born: Cefneithin, Wales, 1945

Country: Wales

Position: Fly-half

International caps: 25

Clubs: Llanelli, Cardiff

Representative honours: British Lions, Barbarians

Zealand, masterminded by the same Carwyn James whom John had studied as a youth. John's brilliant tactical kicking demoralised the All Blacks in the first Test at Dunedin, none more so than their full-back Fergie McCormick. Prior to the match, he was the man the Lions feared most but John totally destroyed McCormick's confidence with a succession of garryowens and tantalising kicks that found touch just out of the full-back's reach. By the end of the game McCormick was a broken man and didn't play in another Test. John never looked back after that, scoring a crucial try and drop goal in the third Test, eventually finishing with 30 points in the series and a record 180 points on the tour. King John was the toast of the British Isles.

A year later came the bombshell. At the age of 27 and with the world at his feet, Barry John suddenly announced his retirement. His final game for Wales was a 20-6 victory over France, ensuring that he bowed out where he had spent the last few years – at the top.

Phil Bennett once described Barry John as 'a one-off genius.' Like New Zealanders, Bennett was not prone to wild exaggeration.

A rare mis-feed – the ball is knocked out of Gareth Edwards' hands as he attempts to feed Barry John

JACK KYLE

Hailed as the finest fly-half in the world, Jack Kyle earned 46 international caps for Ireland

Jack Kyle

Born: Belfast, Northern Ireland, 1926

Country: Ireland

Position: Fly-half

International caps: 46

Clubs: Queen's University

Province/District: Ulster, British Lions, Barbarians

JACK KYLE

Just as the Welsh still worship the ground that Barry John used to walk on, so the Irish fondly recall their own star fly-half, Jack Kyle, the driving force behind their only Grand Slam, way back in 1948. No wonder the Irish took him to their hearts. Not only was he a supremely talented and courageous player, hurling his slight frame into bone-crunching tackles, he also possessed some of those endearing Irish qualities. He once turned up for an international match practice with only one boot and had to admit to the Ireland coach that he had forgotten to bring the right one.

When he did remember both boots, Kyle used them to great effect, summoning the strength to propel mighty punts downfield, which in a flash turned desperate defence into promising attack. His trademark was the finely judged diagonal kick for his threequarters to run onto, placed so as to cause maximum discomfort to the opposition full-backs. Like all great fly-halves he had that knack of being able to spot a gap, which he would instantly exploit either with a shrewd kick or a jinking, darting run. Watching the diminutive Kyle weaving his way through the ranks of opposing forwards in those post-war years must have been like seeing a small boy chased by the Keystone Cops.

John Wilson Kyle played his early rugby for Queen's University, Belfast, where he was studying medicine. He first arrived on the international scene in 1946, appearing for the national side in the 'Victory' Tests for which caps were not awarded. He made his official Ireland debut the following year in a 12-8 defeat to France in Dublin but within 12 months his match-winning brilliance and infectious enthusiasm had inspired his country to their greatest-ever season, the Grand Slam sealed with a hard-fought 6-3 victory over Wales in Belfast. That night the pocket Ulsterman was the toast of all Ireland.

The Irish almost repeated the feat the next year, only to be thwarted by a 16-9 defeat to France, and consequently they had to settle for the Triple Crown. Wales interrupted the Irish run in 1950 but a third title in four years was captured in 1951 when only a draw in Cardiff deprived Ireland of another Triple Crown. By then Kyle was acknowledged as the finest fly-half in the world, his reputation augmented by his performances on the Lions' tour to New Zealand and Australia in 1950 when he won widespread praise for his technical skills and sportsmanship. The tourists' back division, with Kyle at its heart, provided tremendous entertainment throughout the tour but the pack proved no match for the Kiwis, as a result of which three of the four

Tests in New Zealand were lost. The Australian leg proved more successful, both Tests ending in wins for the Lions with Kyle scoring one of five tries in the 24-3 triumph in Sydney. In total he played in nineteen of the matches on the tour (including all six Tests), going over for seven tries himself and creating many more for his team-mates.

Although Kyle was never again selected for the Lions, he played on for Ireland for another eight years. He gained his fiftieth international cap (including Lions' matches) in the 9-6 victory over Australia at Lansdowne Road in 1958 – the first time Ireland had beaten a touring side. Two games later he hung up his boots (both of them) after a 12-6 win over Scotland, his 46 Irish caps creating a new world record. Incidentally, in eleven matches against Scotland he never once finished on the losing side, having been absent for the Scots' 1955 win at Murrayfield.

A deeply religious man, Jack Kyle later lived and worked in Kenya and was awarded the OBE. Nearly 50 years after he last wore the green shirt, he remains a true hero of Irish rugby.

JONAH LOMU

Nothing could stop the headlong charge of Jonah Lomu, except a rare kidney disease

A raw young talent burst onto the scene at the 1995 World Cup in South Africa and within a matter of three weeks had become the sport's first true superstar. That was how long it took Jonah Lomu, a 20-year-old winger from Auckland, to steamroller the defences of Ireland, Wales, Scotland and England. With each game of the tournament, his reputation multiplied ten-fold so that by the time New Zealand came to face England in the semi-finals, their players knew what to expect from this awesome phenomenon. But that didn't mean they could stop him. Brushing aside tackles like a man swatting flies, Lomu used his irresistible combination of pace and power to demolish the English as he ran in four brilliant tries – the first All Black since 1905 to cross the line four times in a Test against England. Although New Zealand lost the final in a match dominated by the boot, it came as no surprise when Lomu was voted Player of the Tournament. There could really have been no other choice. We were in the presence of genius.

A New Zealander of Tongan descent, Lomu grew up in the tough suburbs of South Auckland. As a boy he represented Auckland Primary Schools at Rugby League, using his pace to devastating effect, as well as excelling at track and field. When he was fourteen he switched codes to Rugby Union and became a star player with Wesley College's First XV, operating as a giant, mobile loose forward over a period of five years. He regularly played in area age-grade matches and in season 1991-92 he locked the New Zealand Secondary Schools scrum before moving to No. 8 for the same team the following year. He finished both seasons as the top try scorer.

Although Lomu was clearly a young man of enormous potential, his unique talents had yet to grace a national stage. That situation was rectified in 1994 when, in his first year out of school, he took the Hong Kong Sevens tournament by storm. As one scribe noted: 'New Zealand rugby fans had never seen such a breathtaking combination of speed, power, ball skills and amazing tackle-breaking.' In May of that year he made his debut for Counties in the unfamiliar position of wing. The switch proved an inspired move, Lomu racing to three tries. The selectors began to sit up and take notice and, at the age of nineteen years 45 days, Jonah Lomu became the youngest-ever All Black Test player when he took to the field against France at Christchurch on 26 June 1994.

So to the 1995 World Cup. Standing 6ft 5in tall and weighing nineteen stone, Lomu made most of his opponents look like friends of Snow White. He went over for seven tries in total, including some of the best running scores ever seen in the game of rugby.

Whereas the opposition was unable to stop him, illness could and in 1996 he was diagnosed with a rare kidney disorder, forcing him to put his playing career on hold. However, he bounced back with a vengeance, returning to the All Black side at the end of 1997 and winning a gold medal in the rugby sevens at the 1998 Commonwealth Games in Kuala Lumpur. At the 1999 World Cup he scored a record eight tries (crossing the line in five successive matches) and his career total of fifteen World Cup tries is also a tournament record. The youngest player in the world to have scored ten Test match tries and the first player in the world to have scored twelve Test match tries in a calendar year, Lomu is already the third most prolific Test try-scorer in All Black history with 37 up to the end of 2002. In every sense of the word Jonah Lomu is a true giant of rugby.

Jonah Lomu

Born: Auckland, New Zealand, 1975

Country: New Zealand

Position: Wing

International caps: 63

Clubs: Wesley College

Province/District: Counties Manukau, Wellington, Barbarians

GREAT RUGBY HEROES

JONAH LOMU

MICHAEL LYNAGH

MICHAEL LYNAGH

W hen Michael Lynagh retired from international rugby after his country's disappointing quarter-final defeat to England at the 1995 World Cup, the Australian captain admitted that his exit had not exactly gone according to the script. 'It had to end one day,' he said, 'and today's the day. I won't be coming off the field all sweaty and bruised and holding up a trophy, but . . .'

It was a low-key end to a career that had seen the Brisbane-born Lynagh create a new world international points record of 911 (before it was passed by Wales's Neil Jenkins in 1999) and a new points record for Queensland of 1,166. He also set new Australian standards for the number of conversions in Tests (140) and penalties (177).

Nicknamed 'Noddy', Australia's most-capped fly-half made his international debut against Fiji in 1984 but because of the presence of Mark Ella, he had to play his first five Tests at inside centre. He demonstrated his kicking abilities with three penalties on a mudheap of a pitch but did not take over the role on a regular basis until the tour of the UK where he scored 21 points against Scotland to equal Paul McLean's national record. Then when Mark Ella retired, Lynagh inherited the fly-half spot and quickly broke the Australian record with 23 points against Canada.

Thereafter Lynagh formed part of the so-called 'Holy Trinity' with scrum-half Nick Farr-Jones and winger David Campese. Between them they were responsible for Australia's success in years to come although the first World Cup ended in a surprising semi-final defeat to France. Lynagh scored sixteen points in that match and 82 in the tournament's six games and was again outstanding in defeat when the Lions visited in 1989. The following year he broke his own Australian record with 24 points in the second Test against France (including two tries) and his eleven points in the third Test enabled him to become the first player in history to pass the 500-points mark in internationals.

After missing a crucial last-minute penalty against New Zealand in the 1991 Bledisloe Cup, Lynagh redeemed himself against Ireland in the World Cup quarter-finals. With Farr-Jones off injured and the Wallabies looking a beaten side, Lynagh grabbed the captain's armband and inspired an epic fightback. As Australia poured forward in a bid to save the match, he boldly told his men to ignore a drop goal that would level the scores in favour of the possibility of a match-winning try. Fittingly it was Lynagh himself who dived over for the last-ditch winner. New Zealand were duly dispatched in the semi-finals and, overcoming

Michael Lynagh

Born: Brisbane, Australia, 1963

Country: Australia

Position: Centre, fly-half

International caps: 72

Clubs: University of Queensland, Saracens

Province/District: Queensland, Barbarians

a crisis of confidence in his kicking, Lynagh scored seven points in the final to see Australia home 12-6 against England.

Appointed Australian captain in 1993, Lynagh had now added adventurous attacking runs to his kicking game, illustrated by the fact that he managed seventeen Test tries compared to the one scored by his All Black counterpart Grant Fox. However, he was at his best when providing telling passes for the likes of Campese.

In 1995 Lynagh appeared in his third World Cup but, despite scoring a try in the opening match with South Africa, was unable to urge his team on to greater efforts and they eventually succumbed to England in what would be his last international.

Although Lynagh

continued to play at club level for Saracens in the English Premiership, his retirement threatened to leave a sizeable hole in the Australian team. The *Brisbane Courier Mail* wrote: 'Like Bradman, Lynagh will be sorely missed. There is no heir apparent. In many respects Lynagh embodied the best of his two brilliant predecessors, the kicking game of Paul McLean and the running game – when he chose to reveal it – of Mark Ella. Such a player will not be easily replaced.'

Michael Lynagh's goal-kicking skill led him to become the first player in history to score over 500 points in internationals

WILLIE JOHN McBRIDE

Aggressive, uncompromising and ruthless, Willie John McBride also won the genteel Pipesmoker of the Year Award

Willie John McBride

Born: Toombridge, Northern Ireland, 1940

Country: Ireland

Position: Lock

International caps: 63

Clubs: Ballymena

Representative honours: Ulster, British Lions, Barbarians

WILLIE JOHN McBRIDE

Willie John McBride took fewer prisoners than Inspector Clouseau. A man mountain at 6ft 3in tall and weighing seventeen stone, he relished the physical aspect of the game, invariably operating on the basis that it was always best to get your retaliation in first. To be brutally honest – and McBride could be both brutal and honest — as a lineout jumper or runner with the ball he was nothing particularly special but he was a formidable mauler and scrummager and as a leader of men he was beyond compare.

Never was this more evident than on the 1974 Lions' tour to South Africa when McBride, as captain, set out to ensure that his team would not be intimidated by the snarling Springbok forwards. Previous Lions had rolled over in the face of South African aggression but McBride was hell bent on fighting fire with fire and did it so effectively that the tourists won 21 out of 22 matches, drawing only the last game. The battered hosts were left in awe of the bruising Brits and the legend of Willie John McBride was born, to be preserved for future generations.

The McBride story began on a farm some 30 miles from Belfast. His father died when Willie John was just five, as a result of which the remaining family all had to muck in together to keep the farm going. This left precious little time for sport and it was not until the age of seventeen that Willie John first played rugby, taking up the game in his final years at Ballymena Academy. His powerful build made him a natural forward and, after serving his apprenticeship with Ulster, he appeared for the national side in 1962, making his debut against England at Twickenham, a match that the home team won 16-0. Despite this and other disappointing results for the Irish, McBride was chosen at the end of the season for the Lions' tour of South Africa. It proved another salutary lesson. He played in the last two Tests but finished on the losing side in both.

It was the 1966 tour of New Zealand that moulded McBride's philosophy. All four Tests were lost but the Ulsterman left his mark on his redoubtable opposite number, Colin Meads, who claimed that a punch from McBride was the hardest he had ever received. After that particular fracas, the two men developed a healthy respect for each other. McBride showed no such respect for a one-eyed South African forward, Johann de Bruyn, whom he encountered on that infamous 1974 tour. After being repeatedly outgunned in the lineout by the man with a glass eye, McBride apparently gave orders for de Bruyn to be hit in his good eye. It was all within the laws of the game ... at least the laws according to Willie John McBride.

That was McBride's record fifth and final Lions' tour, following on the heels of trips to South Africa in 1968 and New Zealand in 1971 where he outshone the venerable Meads. McBride raised combative forward play to new heights, ensuring that the tourists could hold their own in any brawl. Above all, he was a supreme motivator, constantly encouraging those around him. In return they gave him unquestioning loyalty and maximum effort. The Lions have never had a more inspirational captain.

His playing career finished in 1975 with a record number of Irish caps and in his final match – against France in Dublin – he brought the house down by scoring his only try for Ireland. He later managed the 1983 Lions' tour of New Zealand and, perhaps to the surprise of those who had faced him in a loose maul, won that most laid-back of awards, Pipesmoker of the Year. People may still debate his merits as a player but there is one thing about which everyone is agreed: Willie John McBride was a good man to have on your side.

COLIN MEADS

Apart from Willie John McBride, nobody messed with Colin Meads . . . or if they did they quickly came to regret it. At 6ft 4in tall, Meads was built like a bear and had the attitude of one with a permanently sore head. A farmer from King Country in the rural heart of New Zealand, it is said that he trained for rugby by running up hills near his home with a sheep tucked under each arm. When Springbok centre John Gainsford had the effrontery to tangle with him on the field of play, he described Meads' grip as 'like being held by a band of steel.' It was a lesson learned.

With the possible exception of the Godfather, Meads was the last person in the world to try and intimidate. Apart from the sheer physical risk, it was an impossible task because Meads had such mental strength that he feared no one. It would take more than a sly punch or bite to put him off his game; on the contrary it would simply spur him on to greater efforts. For this most mobile of forwards was also a clever footballer who enjoyed a record-equalling fifteen seasons as an All Black.

After representing King Country at junior level, he made his senior debut as a nineteen-year-old against South Auckland Counties in 1955, marking his debut not only with a try but a perfectly executed dropped goal. He impressed sufficiently to tour Australia and Ceylon with New Zealand Colts later that season. Selection for the All Blacks was inevitable and it duly arrived in 1957 on the tour to Australia where he played in both internationals. In the second of those matches he scored his first Test try while deputising for Frank McMullen in the unfamiliar position of wing.

Once in the side there was no shifting Meads although, particularly in the early days, he alternated between lock, flanker and No.8. However, a disastrous 20-5 defeat to Australia in the third Test of 1964 saw him switch permanently back to lock. On 14 occasions he played alongside his younger brother Stan, whom Colin regarded as the best of his locking partners. Their finest hour together in an All Black shirt came against the 1966 British Lions, a series that New Zealand won 4-0 – the first time the Lions had suffered a series whitewash. With players such as Brian Lochore, Chris Laidlaw and Kel Tremain, the All Blacks were an awesome unit in the 1960s and nobody lived up to that tag more than Meads.

If Meads occasionally contravened the laws on the pitch, he was a fine sportsman off it and was hugely respected by team-mates and opponents alike. Even after he had made the wrong sort of headlines by being sent off against Scotland in 1967 – only the second player in history to be ordered off in a full international — he continued to exchange Christmas cards with the referee in question, Ireland's Ken Kelleher, for over 20 years.

Meads' playing career ended on a low note in 1971 as he manfully tried – but ultimately failed – to hold together a young New Zealand side against a rampant Lions. After coaching King Country from 1976-81, he became a selector first for North Island and then for the national team, only to be voted off the panel in 1986 for coaching the rebel New Zealand Cavaliers side in South Africa. His view was that politics had no right to interfere with the game he loved.

'Pine Tree' Meads remains a cult hero. His own fan club still meets on a regular basis, each member wearing a No. 5 jersey, downing beers and reading excerpts from Meads' autobiography.

In 1999 the man once described by McBride as being 'as hard as the hobs of hell' was named Player of the Century at the New Zealand Rugby Football Union awards dinner. Few would argue with his selection . . . and certainly not to his face.

GREAT RUGBY HEROES

COLIN MEADS

Colin Meads feared no one but had a healthy respect for Willie John McBride's right hook

Colin Meads

Born: Cambridge, New Zealand, 1936

Country: New Zealand
Position: Flanker, No 8, lock

International caps: 55

Clubs: Waitete

Province/District: King Country, North Island

GRAHAM MOURIE

GRAHAM MOURIE

Graham Mourie's attitude to playing was straightforward. 'The whole basis is enjoyment. The more often you win, the greater the enjoyment, but never a win at all costs.'

It was a philosophy to which Mourie adhered throughout his playing career and helped make the Taranaki flanker one of the most respected captains in All Black history. Sure, he played hard and he played to win, but he also ensured that committed play never crossed that dangerous boundary into becoming dirty play. A fearless tackler, he was an inspiration to his players and had the priceless knack of invariably being able to extract a full 80-minute performance from them. There was no room for slacking or showboating with Mourie.

His potential both as a player and a future leader was evident from an early age. He led a schoolboy team on a tour of Australia and later represented New Zealand Colts, New Zealand Universities and Wellington province while completing his studies. In 1975 he captained New Zealand Juniors against the Romanian tourists, scoring his team's two tries in a 10-10 draw. The senior selectors had been consistently monitoring his progress and decided to name him as captain of the New Zealand 'B' team that went to Argentina in 1976. He emerged from such a baptism of fire with his reputation enhanced. The team returned unbeaten and the coach, Jack Gleeson, said of Mourie: 'This young man has a great future as New Zealand's captain.'

The following year he won his first full cap against Phil Bennett's Lions, playing in the final two Tests at Dunedin and Auckland, which the All Blacks won 19-7 and 10-9 respectively. At the end of 1977 he was appointed captain of the New Zealand team to tour Italy and France. After appearing in both Tests, Mourie returned to France for the northern season and played for the Paris University club. A back injury ruled him out of the home series against the 1978 Wallabies (although he was a reserve in the final Test), but he resumed the captaincy for the tour of Britain and Ireland at the end of the year, which saw the All Blacks complete the Grand Slam of the four Home Unions for the first time. Mourie's dynamic play and intelligent captaincy earned him the Player of the Year award from *Rothmans Rugby Yearbook*.

Despite having to miss the 1980 tour of Australia and Fiji because of farming commitments, Mourie led the side to face Scotland in 1981, maintaining his proud tradition of never losing against a team from the British Isles in eleven encounters. Mourie remained a man of principle, even if it threatened to jeopardise his career, and later in 1981

Graham Mourie

Born: Opunake, New Zealand, 1952

Country: New Zealand

Position: Flanker

International caps: 21

Clubs: Opunake, Paris University

Representative honours: Taranaki, Wellington, Barbarians he caused a storm by declaring himself unavailable for selection against the visiting South Africans. He strongly opposed that controversial tour and won more friends by taking such a firm moral stance.

He returned to lead the All Blacks in Romania and France and captained the side that regained the Bledisloe Cup from Australia in 1982, after which he returned to France for another club season. Then he caused another stir over the publication of his autobiography, not as a result of the content but because he insisted that, by accepting payment for the book, he was therefore a professional. The NZRFU promptly banned him.

His playing career over, he coached the Coastal club in Taranaki and in 1994 stood unsuccessfully to be a New Zealand selector. Following a stint as coach of Wellington, he took up a similar post in 1999 with the local Super 12 team, the Hurricanes, remaining there until the end of the 2002 season despite meeting with only limited success. In 2003 Mourie was elected as a director of the New Zealand Rugby Football Board. This most honest and fair-minded of men will once again have the opportunity to influence the game in his native country.

Graham Mourie never shied away from controversy, refusing to play against South Africa and publishing a book that led to him being banned

HENNIE MULLER

HENNIE MULLER

Hennie Muller's reputation as the outstanding No.8 in the history of Springbok rugby was built on a 1949 whitewash of the visiting All Blacks. He won his first cap – at the advanced age of 27 – in the opening Test of that tour and was hugely instrumental in South Africa's 4-0 series triumph, having been ordered to unsettle the All Black midfield players and make their lives a misery. Through gritted teeth (that's if they had any left after a Muller tackle), the vanquished All Blacks called him 'a genius in the loose' and 'a menace of menaces'. They just wished he had been on their side.

Muller's marauding in the loose and crunching tackles made him a feared adversary. No opponent was safe when he was on the prowl. He was invariably first to reach any breakdown and was easily fast enough to have been a threequarter, but chose to remain in the pack. Standing 6ft tall, he was compared to a lean and hungry greyhound in pursuit of the hare, hence the nickname given to him by Dr Danie Craven of 'Windhond' – 'the greyhound of the Veldt'. There may have been bigger men in the pack but none as strong as Muller who acquired his toughness from working in a gold mine near Boksburg. Writer Norman Canale described Muller's impact on that All Black tour: 'There was invariably a hum of expectancy in the crowd as Hennie stood at the back of the lineout in that characteristic hands-on-hips pose, his distinctive blond hair a spotlight, his eyes darting warnings at the opposing fly-half, already twitchy at the menace lurking close by.'

Bob Scott, the All Black full-back, later wrote of Muller's intimidating performance: 'So long as he stopped an All Black, that was all that mattered; what happened to himself was of no importance. I doubt rugby will ever see Muller's likes again. He is as fast as a track sprinter and as alert and as hungry as a hawk. And on top of everything he is completely fearless and quite ruthless.'

Muller was such a fierce competitor that he used to stop talking to his wife three days before a big Test because he was too busy mentally scoring tries in his head to bother with idle chitchat. Yet the cold-eyed destroyer on the pitch was an emotional man off it and wept with pride in the dressing-room after Scotland had been routed 44-0 in 1951 in what became known as 'The Murrayfield Massacre'. Muller had inherited the captaincy on that tour following a serious eye injury to Basil Kenyon and proceeded to lead the Springboks to victories in 30 out of 31 matches, including wins against all of the five nations. Their only defeat came at the hands of London Counties. Muller himself

Hennie Muller

Born: Witbank, South Africa, 1922 (d. 1977)

Country: South Africa

Position: No 8

International caps: 13

Province/District: Transvaal

weighed in with Test tries against Scotland and France while his conversion and penalty settled a close encounter with England 8-3 in the Springboks' favour. Of the thirteen Tests he played between 1949 and 1953, he was on the losing side only once – against Australia at Cape Town. However, the Springboks still won that series 3-1 to confirm their status as the best side in the world.

A kind and compassionate man, Hennie Muller loved to spread the gospel of rugby and impart his experiences to others. He died at the age of 55 while addressing a primary school in Cape Town. In a tribute Dr Craven said: 'Hennie Muller was probably the fastest Springbok I have ever seen. He was finely strung and emotional, a strong man who nevertheless could and did cry tears of sorrow and joy. Hennie, without any doubt, was one of the greatest players the world has seen.'

The Springboks line up for the 1952 Test against England at Twickenham. Hennie Muller is seated in the middle row fourth from left

TONY O'REILLY

It could only have happened to Tony O'Reilly. Seven years after winning his last cap for Ireland, he was on a 1970 business trip to London when he was awarded a shock recall to the side after being told that right-wing Bill Brown had injured himself in training prior to the forthcoming international at Twickenham. Never one to reject his country in their hour of need, O'Reilly agreed to take Brown's place, arriving at Twickenham in a chauffeur-driven Rolls-Royce. Hopelessly overweight – it was suggested that the England wing would have to make a lengthy detour just to get round him – and perilously unfit, he contributed precious little to the game except to add to the legend that is Dr Anthony Joseph Francis Kevin O'Reilly, wealthy businessman and rugby player extraordinary.

O'Reilly has been the subject of almost as many stories as the Blarney Stone. But to file him solely under 'colourful character' would

Tony O'Reilly on British Lions duty in the 1950s. He is now one of Ireland's wealthiest men

be to overlook a substantial playing career, which saw him burst onto the scene as a teenage prodigy and go on to score a record number of tries for the British Lions. He has been hailed as one of the best Irish backs of all time and certainly South African rugby fans reckoned they had never seen a livelier winger.

His rise to international status was little short of meteoric. At eighteen, he had only just broken into the Old Belvedere First XV when, in January 1955, he was included in the Ireland team to play France. Within another six months he was playing in his first Test for the Lions. At 6ft 2in and fifteen stone, his powerful running made an explosive impact. In the first Test at Johannesburg he created one try for Jim Greenwood and then sprinted over for a touchdown himself to seal the Lions' 23-22 victory. For the final Test at Port Elizabeth he was surprisingly chosen at centre but still managed to score the final try of the drawn series, although he also succeeded in dislocating his shoulder in the process. His total of sixteen tries on the tour earned him the undying admiration of the South African fans.

It also won him the approval of the Lions' selectors who sent him abroad again in 1959, this time on the trip to Australia, New Zealand and Canada. After scoring a try in both of the Test victories over Australia, he picked up two more in the 3-1 series defeat to New Zealand. More importantly, his 22 tries on the tour took his Lions' tally to 38, a total that may never be beaten. He played all of these Tests on the wing yet he himself preferred to play as a centre and often persuaded the Irish selectors to field him in that position. Sadly, he never truly fulfilled his potential inside and most observers of the day considered that his talents were better employed out wide. It was a debate that rumbled on for much of his career.

O'Reilly was more than just a great player on tour, he was also great company – an energetic personality, devastating mimic and witty raconteur who was immensely popular with team-mates and opponents alike. Intelligent, handsome and athletic, he was even said to have been offered the title role in the remake of *Ben Hur* but politely declined.

His best rugby was undoubtedly played for the Lions, his Irish appearances being restricted by injuries and growing business commitments. He played what he thought was his last international in 1963, against Wales, quitting the international circus at 26 in order to devote his energies to his commercial work. He was appointed chief executive of the Irish Dairy Marketing Board before he was 30 and later became managing director of Heinz Foods as well as a newspaper magnate. All in all, it's been quite a life.

GREAT RUGBY HEROES

TONY O'REILLY

Tony O'Reilly

Born: Dublin, Eire, 1936

Country: Ireland

Position: Centre, wing

International caps: 29

Clubs: Old Belvedere, Leicester

Representative honours: British Lions, Barbarians

FRANCOIS PIENAAR

Saracens player/coach
Francois Pienaar raises the
Tetley's Bitter Trophy in 1998

Francois Pienaar

Born: Vereeniging, South Africa, 1967

Country: South Africa

Position: Flanker

International caps: 29

Clubs: Rand Afrikaans University, Saracens

Province/District: Transvaal

Representative honours: Barbarians

FRANCOIS PIENAAR

In his foreword to Francois Pienaar's autobiography, Nelson Mandela wrote of the South African captain: 'It was under his inspiring leadership that rugby, a sport previously associated with one sector of our population and with a particular brand of politics, became the pride of the entire country.' Pienaar is one of post-apartheid South Africa's most famous sporting figures, his influence stretching far beyond the rugby field to the black townships. He symbolises the new acceptable face of South Africa, a nation ready to embrace all cultures and all colours.

Pienaar's crowning glory was leading his country to an emotional triumph in the 1995 World Cup. While the squad included only one black player, Chester Williams, the Springboks represented what Archbishop Desmond Tutu had famously called the new Rainbow Nation of South Africa, instead of merely an Afrikaner minority. After New Zealand had been defeated in the final at Ellis Park, Johannesburg, courtesy of an extra-time drop goal from Joel Stransky, the Webb Ellis Trophy was presented to the captain by Mandela, wearing a Springbok jersey bearing Pienaar's number. Just as Mandela had urged black South Africans to support the team, Pienaar, in his acceptance speech, said that the victory was 'for all 43 million South Africans'. It was among the most poignant moments in the history of South African sport.

Pienaar was born into a working-class Afrikaner family in Vereeniging and soon excelled at a variety of sports, eventually winning an athletic scholarship to Rand Afrikaans University in Johannesburg where he read law. A promising rugby player he set himself the goal of playing provincial rugby for Transvaal and often used to watch the Transvaal side train before returning alone the following day to practise the same routines as the players. His dedication paid off in 1989 when he made his provincial debut. He ultimately made 100 appearances for Transvaal, captaining them on 89 occasions.

When South Africa returned to international competition in 1992, the team performed so poorly that captain Naas Botha retired and Pienaar was called up to lead the team in his first Tests the following summer. The two Tests against France ended in a draw and a single-point defeat but Pienaar retained both his place and the captaincy and within eighteen months had been voted International Player of the Year by *Rugby World* magazine.

The 1995 World Cup led to further personal honours. He was voted

Rugby Personality of the Year by Britain's Rugby Union Writers' Club as well as Newsmaker of the Year in South Africa. However the fairytale was about to end in acrimony when, after leaving the field injured in a Tri-Nations match against the All Blacks in Cape Town, Pienaar was accused by South African coach André Markgraaf of feigning injury. Only fifteen months after lifting the World Cup and helping to unite a nation, Pienaar found himself dropped. The controversy subsequently rebounded on Markgraaf who was axed following the release of a tape on which he could be heard making racist remarks. Pienaar was offered his job back but, upset at his treatment, declined and instead took advantage of the new professional era to join struggling London club Saracens as player/coach. Pienaar immediately transformed Saracens' fortunes and in 1998 guided them to victory over Wasps in the Tetley's Bitter Cup and second spot in the Zurich Premiership. Two years later he retired as a player and became the club's chief executive but when Saracens' form dipped badly in 2001-2 to the extent that they faced a relegation battle, Pienaar decided to return to South Africa.

Francois Pienaar may have left South Africa in contentious circumstances but nobody has forgotten the tremendous ambassadorial work he did in the 1990s. Appropriately, one of his sons has Nelson Mandela for a godfather.

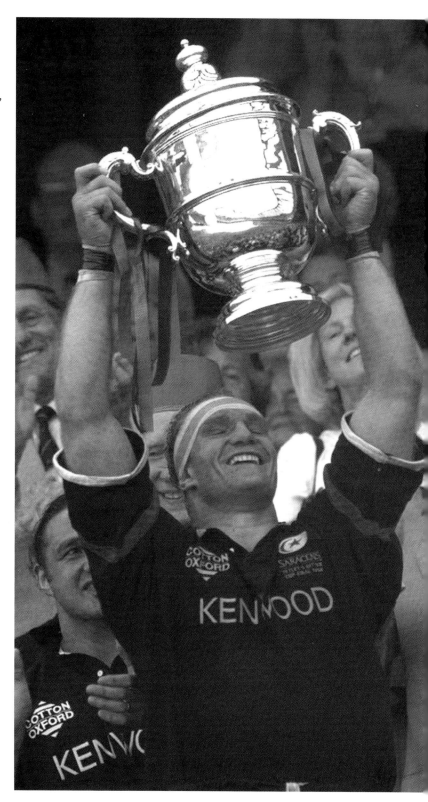

GREAT RUGBY HEROES

HUGO PORTA

HUGO PORTA

Nobody did more to turn Argentina into serious players in world rugby than their brilliant fly-half Hugo Porta. Over a period of 20 seasons he almost single-handedly carried Argentine rugby, lifting the Pumas from a position way down on the second tier to one where they could compete with – and occasionally beat – the best in the world.

Yet Porta could easily have been a professional footballer instead, sharing the short, stocky build, the sudden acceleration, the tenacity, not to mention the handling ability, of Diego Maradona. Educated at a monastery school in Buenos Aires, Porta was courted by Maradona's club, Boca Juniors, but decided to follow his father's advice and study law. That allowed him to concentrate on rugby and, after starting out as a scrum-half, this talented all-round sportsman made his international debut at stand-off against Chile in 1971.

Winning the South American Championship with monotonous regularity, the Pumas began to set their sights further afield and it was Porta, an architect by profession, who drew up the blueprint for international success. In 1976 they put up a plucky performance against a visiting New Zealand XV and in the same year ran Wales mighty close in Cardiff, the Welsh scraping through 19-18 thanks to a last-gasp penalty by Phil Bennett. Then, in 1977, Porta kicked all his country's points in an 18-18 draw with France, who won the Grand Slam that year. In 1978 it was England's turn to face the little man. By now the Argentine forwards had got their game together to complement Porta's tactical kicking and incisive running with the result that England were held to a 13-13 draw at Twickenham, the Pumas scoring two tries in the process. The following year Australia suffered a shock 24-13 defeat in Buenos Aires, Porta making full use of the possession won by his forwards to collect sixteen points, including three dropped goals. Although Australia narrowly won the second Test, Argentina were beginning to be taken seriously.

In 1980, while touring with the South American Jaguars in South Africa, Porta was invited to play for the South African Barbarians against the British Lions. Despite finishing on the losing side, Porta impressed many onlookers, among them legendary Lions' coach Carwyn James who was covering the game for the media. James wrote: 'Everything that happened around Hugo Porta was contested at a much lower level of skill and intellectual awareness. For a critic or coach or ex fly-half, it was a question of having one's faith restored in the aesthetic and artistic possibilities of back play.'

Hugo Porta

Born: Buenos Aires, Argentina, 1951

Country: Argentina

Position: Fly-half

International caps: 58

Clubs: Banco Nacion

Representative honours: South American Jaguars, South African Barbarians

Porta's fame continued to spread and in 1982, a season in which he scored a national record 302 points for his club Banco Nacion, he played probably his finest game at international level, spurring the South American Jaguars to a famous 21-14 victory over a strong Springbok side in Bloemfontein. Porta scored all 21 points – a try, a conversion, a drop goal and four penalties. A year later Porta's Argentina crushed Australia 18-3 in Brisbane and in 1985 beat France 24-16 in Buenos Aires – the Pumas' first victory over the French in sixteen attempts. Another creditable draw, this time against the All Blacks, led to great expectations for the first World Cup but Argentina under-achieved and Porta announced his retirement after the tournament. However, he was tempted back in 1990 when, at the age of 38, he joined the Argentina team that toured the UK. Although he showed flashes of the old magic there was to be no happy ending, his final match being a 49-3 drubbing by Scotland.

Argentina's finest ever player finished with a total of 590 points in Tests, including a world record 28 dropped goals. He later became his country's minister of sport and ambassador to South Africa.

Hugo Porta is the finest rugby player Argentina has ever produced, but he could easily have turned his talents to soccer

GRAHAM PRICE

The cornerstone of the Welsh pack, Price was a tenacious scrummager and safe handler

Entertainer Max Boyce used to call them the 'Viet Gwent' – that famed Pontypool, Wales and British Lions' front row of Graham Price, Bobby Windsor and Charlie Faulkner. Going into battle together for club and country, they performed such heroic feats that an entire legend was built up around their exploits. Although Price was the junior partner, it was he who would go on to enjoy the most distinguished career and when he retired in 1983 he was Wales's most capped prop forward.

It is said that the legend of the Pontypool front row was born not in Gwent but in Paris on an afternoon in 1975 when Price and Faulkner were awarded new caps alongside old hand Windsor. The trio were in awesome form that day, hounding the French into uncharacteristic errors, culminating in a late blunder by bulky No. 8, Jean-Pierre Bastiat, who spilled the ball just outside the Welsh 22. Price was on to the loose ball in a flash and ran 70 metres in stamina-sapping ground before touching down for the try that sealed a 25-10 triumph.

That score not only

illustrated Price's amazing fitness but also his tremendous resolve as he developed into the finest British tight-head of modern times. The cornerstone of the Welsh pack, he was a tenacious scrummager and a safe handler whose run of twelve consecutive appearances for the Lions in Tests set a new record for a front-row forward. He was never better than in adversity. When Paul Ringer was sent off early in the game at Twickenham in 1980, the Welsh pack were left a man short for the remaining 65 minutes. Price rose to the occasion, manning the barricades so effectively that England only scraped home by a single point. Although no one was more committed to the cause than Price, his determination to repel the opposition never transgressed the laws of the game. He played hard but he played fair – even if the same courtesy was not always afforded to him, as in 1978 when a punch thrown by Australia's Steve Finnane broke Price's jaw.

Price was educated at West Monmouth Grammar School and followed two other former pupils, winger Ken J. Jones and hooker Bryn Meredith, into the Welsh and Lions' line-ups. After that eventful international debut against France, Price bedded down into the Wales side, becoming a stalwart for the next eight years. The Pontypool front row joined forces for the Lions on the 1977 tour of New Zealand, playing together against the Counties, Bay of Plenty and Fiji. Price played in all four Tests and Windsor one, but Faulkner missed out. Price's remarkable consistency and durability earned him another Lions' tour in 1980 to South Africa where once again he appeared in all four Tests, but even his try in the opening international at Cape Town wasn't enough to prevent the Lions slipping to a 26-22 defeat. They ended up losing the series 3-1. Three years later he returned to New Zealand and maintained his 100 per cent record by featuring in every one of the four Tests, only to finish on the losing side each time.

Price decided to retire from international rugby at the end of that tour, his last international for Wales having been a 16-9 defeat in Paris. However he continued to play for his beloved Pontypool, totalling over 500 games for the club and turning out against the touring All Blacks in 1989 at the age of 38. He helped Pontypool to a string of Welsh League and Cup triumphs while at national level he was part of the Wales side that won four Triple Crowns and two Grand Slams.

Graham Price's tireless endeavours have ensured that he is fondly remembered not just in Wales but throughout the rugby-playing world. And that's more than you can say for Max Boyce.

Graham Price

Born: Egypt, 1951

Country: Wales

Position: Prop

International caps: 41

Clubs: Pontypool

Representative honours:
British Lions, Barbarians

Dean Richards

Born: Nuneaton, England, 1963

Country: England

Position: No. 8

International caps: 48

Clubs: Roanne, Leicester

Representative honours: The Midlands, British Lions, Barbarians

DEAN RICHARDS

Dean Richards may be a hero for England, having won a record total of caps for a Number 8, but at Welford Road, Leicester, his status is positively God-like. He played 314 games for the Tigers, captaining them for four seasons and becoming only the second forward (after David Matthews) to score 100 tries for the club. A dual Pilkington Cup winner, he was part of the team that won League titles in 1988 and 1995, the latter as captain. He retired from playing in 1998 and when coach Bob Dwyer was unceremoniously shown the door, 'Deano' was appointed his successor, promptly masterminding four successive English Premiership titles. He also established Leicester Tigers as kings of Europe, steering them to their first Heineken European Cup triumph, at the expense of Stade Francais in Paris in 2001. The following year the Tigers made history by successfully defending their European title, defeating Munster in Cardiff. Dean Richards was the toast of Leicester.

Born in Nuneaton, Richards won England schoolboy representative honours at lock but soon moved into the back row where he was to make his name. His first club rugby was played in France for Roanne but he returned to England to play for Tigers, making his debut at Neath in 1982. Within a year, he was back in the principality, this time on tour with the Barbarians. England Under-23 honours brought a full cap in March 1986 and he marked the occasion in style, becoming the first England player in 57 years to score two tries on his debut as Ireland were beaten 25-20 at Twickenham.

Although never the quickest of players, the burly policeman soon demonstrated the priceless knack of being able to anticipate where the ball would arrive. Always playing with his socks rolled down, his shambling appearance belied his tactical nous while he used his considerable strength to propel himself into the thick of the action and launch powerful drives, his trademark being the bear-hug tackle whereby he would turn an opponent right round, thus presenting the ball to his own pack. Utterly fearless, time and again he would swallow up the opposition high ball and release it only when he was ready, not a moment earlier. It was on the Lions' tour of Australia in 1989 that he truly came of age, producing a powerhouse performance to enable the Lions to storm to victory in the Second Test in what became known as 'The Battle of Ballymore'.

Sidelined by a shoulder injury in 1990, he returned to help England to the Grand Slam in 1991, only to be surprisingly

GREAT RUGBY HEROES

DEAN RICHARDS

dropped in favour of Mickey Skinner for the World Cup quarter-final against Scotland. He also missed the first two games of the 1992 Five Nations but, after an inspirational appearance as substitute in the Calcutta Cup match, he regained his place for the France and Wales matches as England swept to a second successive Grand Slam. England coach Jack Rowell deemed Richards surplus to requirements in 1993 but the view was not shared by the Lions management and the Leicester man played in all three Tests on that year's tour to New Zealand. Although the series was lost 2-1, Richards gained his revenge when the All Blacks visited the UK. Combining magnificently with Ben Clarke and Tim Rodber, he destroyed the New Zealand pack and drove England to a 15-9 victory. Back in favour, he was part of another memorable match less than a year later when South Africa were crushed 32-15 in Pretoria.

As in his first international, his last opponents – in March 1996 – were Ireland at Twickenham, the 28-15 victory helping England to another Five Nations title. He retired from international rugby with 48 caps and six tries to his name, but as Leicester fans will testify, the best was yet to come.

In the thick of things: Dean Richards directs operations around the scrum, while his England team-mate, Matt Dawson, awaits the Scots' put in

JEAN-PIERRE RIVES

JEAN-PIERRE RIVES

Standing a mere 5ft 10in tall and weighing barely thirteen stone, Jean-Pierre Rives was a pygmy among the beefy French forwards of the seventies and eighties. However he compensated for his relative lack of stature with an iron will to win, launching himself fearlessly into tackles on men nearly twice his size. More often than not such encounters left him with blood streaming down his face and matted to his flowing flaxen hair, but moments later he would be back for more, pummelling opponents for all he was worth in an attempt to win the ball for France. In his book *100 Great Rugby Players* Gareth Edwards summed up the effects of a collision with Rives: 'He was one of those opponents who was not satisfied with a simple tackle, but sought to drive right through you, as if he wanted to pin you to a goal-post.'

Aside from his fierce tackling and intense competitive spirit, Rives was able to bring one other great attribute to forward play – pace. While his burly team-mates lumbered around, the Toulouse flanker possessed a turn of foot that invariably made him the first to arrive at a breakdown. He combined brilliantly with blind-side flanker Jean-Claude Skrela and No. 8 Jean-Pierre Bastiat to spearhead a back row that was the envy of the world and which laid the foundations for France's Grand Slam of 1977. The French fans adored him, not only for his courage against overwhelming odds but also because he had the verve and style that they so admire in their top sportsmen. In recognition of his blond mane, they christened him the 'Casque d'Or' or 'Golden Helmet'. He was the perfect embodiment of Gallic flair.

It is said that Rives was destined to be special, having been born at the stroke of midnight on New Year's Eve 1952. His international career began with a 27-20 victory over England at Twickenham in 1975 and he only tasted defeat twice in his first thirteen games for his country – to Ireland in Dublin and Wales in Cardiff. Like a poor Beaujolais, the French did not always travel well but they were nigh on invincible in their own backyard. However, they overcame their travel sickness in 1977 with that second Grand Slam (the first having been nine years earlier), courtesy of hard-fought victories at Twickenham and Lansdowne Road.

With his familiar blend of tigerish tackling, electrifying pace, smooth distribution and tactical nous, Rives was hugely instrumental in France's whitewash and was rewarded with the captaincy when Bastiat stepped down in 1978. Over the next six years Rives would skipper his country a record 34 times (although the figure was subsequently equalled by Philippe Saint-André in 1997). Leading from the front, Rives

Jean-Pierre Rives

Born: Toulouse, France, 1952

Country: France

Position: Flanker

International caps: 59

Clubs: Toulouse, Racing Club de France

Representative honours: Barbarians

conjured up a memorable 24-19 victory over New Zealand at Auckland in 1979 after the first Test had been lost 23-9, the turnaround in fortunes being an indication of the character he had already engendered in his troops. His determination was infectious. This was further exemplified two years later when he won a second Grand Slam. France went on to share the Five Nations Championship with Ireland in 1983 but his hopes of a third Grand Slam were shattered in 1984 when the Cockerels had their wings clipped 21-12 at Murrayfield. On the back of that defeat, he decided to retire from international rugby. He remains France's most capped flanker.

Rives saw himself as a flamboyant artist on the pitch and has pursued that vision with a new career as a sculptor, working out of a disused railway shed in North Paris and exhibiting as far afield as Mauritius. Asked to explain the connection between sculpture and rugby, he answered: 'Everything is energy. Sculpture is just energy and invention. Rugby is energy – and sometimes invention too.' Very enigmatic. Very Jean-Pierre Rives.

France's most-capped flanker, Jean-Pierre Rives was known as the 'Casque d'Or' or 'Golden Helmet'

PHILIPPE SELLA

PHILIPPE SELLA

Former French coach Jacques Fouroux once described Philippe Sella as having the 'strength of a bull but the touch of a piano player.' This neatly summarises the two very different sides of the world's most-capped rugby player. On the one hand the stocky Sella was a tough competitor, a stalwart in defence, capable of making try-saving tackles; on the other he was a fluent, supercharged runner who could flit through the tiniest gap *en route* to one of the 30 tries he scored for his country.

A model of consistency, Sella scored tries at a steady rate throughout his thirteen years in international rugby. He was also extremely fit, at one stage appearing in 45 consecutive Tests, and helped France to either outright victory or a share in six Five Nations Championships. However the prize of a World Cup winner's medal repeatedly eluded him although he was a beaten finalist in 1987 and a member of the French team that finished third in 1995.

Sella's promise was apparent from his school days. Born in Tonneins in the south-west of France, he made his schoolboy international debut against Scotland and was soon considered good enough for a run-out with his local club, Agen. Apart from an early dalliance with amateur Rugby League in Clairac, he remained loyal to Agen for the remainder of his international career. After learning the ropes with France Colts, French Universities and the France 'B' team, the 20-year-old was called up to the full national side in October 1982 for the match with Romania in Bucharest. Playing on the wing, Sella remembered little of the occasion, ending up in a Bucharest hospital after being concussed. To add insult to injury, France lost 13-9. His second cap was altogether more successful as he scored two tries in a 25-12 victory over Argentina at Toulouse.

A splendid all-round athlete (he even won a clutch of international caps at full-back as well as his 104 at centre), Sella's ability to slice through opposing defences was beginning to make him a real handful. His blistering pace was difficult enough to contain, even without the numerous jinks, dummies and sidesteps that he had added to his repertoire. He had the tricks to go past a defender on the inside and the speed to race clear on the outside. Many a French player has since tried to copy his running style but none has ever bettered it.

In 1984 he scored touchdowns against Ireland, Wales and Scotland but went one better two years later by recording tries against all four countries in the Championship, becoming only the fourth person in

Philippe Sella

Born: Tonneins, France, 1962

Country: France

Position: Centre, full-back

International caps: 111

Clubs: Agen, Saracens

Representative honours: Barbarians

history to do so and only the second Frenchman after Patrick Estève in 1983. Paired with newcomer Denis Charvet of Toulouse, Sella helped France to a Grand Slam in 1987, one of the highlights of which was a 19-15 triumph at Twickenham. Sella was in sensational form that day, crossing the England line for a crucial try at the end of a 70-metre dash – a score that he still rates as his all-time favourite. In the same year France reached the final of the World Cup where they lost 29-9 to hosts New Zealand. The competition brought further disappointment in 1991 with a quarter-final defeat to England, a pain that was only partly soothed by victory over the same opponents in the third place match in 1995. That 19-9 victory in Pretoria was Sella's last international. He subsequently joined Saracens with whom he won the Tetley's Bitter Cup – the last piece of silverware in a glorious career.

But let us not forget Sella's other side, powerfully illustrated during the 1990 Test with Australia when he floored Wallaby lock Peter Fitzsimons with a blow of which Mike Tyson would have been proud. One way or the other, Philippe Sella always left his mark.

Philippe Sella's first international ended in a hospital visit for concussion, but there would be 110 others that he would remember a little better

FERGUS SLATTERY

Fergus Slattery

Born: Dublin, Eire, 1949

Country: Ireland

Position: Flanker

International caps: 61

Clubs: University College Dublin, Blackrock College

Representative honours: British Lions, Barbarians

There were never any half measures where Fergus Slattery was concerned. He put everything into every game, training and performing with a fervour and passion that would earn him an Irish record 61 caps as a flanker (including seventeen as captain) and an international career spanning fourteen years. Of his contemporaries in world rugby, his commitment, aggression, pace and robust tackling were matched only by his French counterpart Jean-Pierre Rives.

An open-side specialist, Slattery was adept at detaching himself quickly from scrummages and then ripping into the opposition fly-half before a break could be made . . . like a lion waiting to pounce on a hesitant gazelle. His covering in defence was outstanding, as was his speed to the breakdown in the loose, but it was his high fitness level and unquenchable spirit that really made him such a valuable player both for Ireland and the British Lions.

He made his international debut as a 20-year-old in an 8-8 draw with the touring South Africans in January 1970 while still an undergraduate at University College, Dublin, and created such a favourable impression that he went on to play in all of Ireland's Five Nations matches that season, in the course of which he helped deny Wales the Triple Crown. His rapid rise to international prominence was confirmed by selection for the 1971 Lions' tour to New Zealand. The Welshman John Taylor occupied the open-side slot for the first two Tests and when Taylor's loss of form did finally present the Dublin auctioneer with a chance, Slattery was struck down with tonsillitis. Taylor kept his place for the final international so that Slattery returned home with just thirteen provincial matches under his belt. Nevertheless, it was all part of his learning curve and the experience gained would be put to good use on the next Lions' tour.

In the meantime Slattery was playing his club rugby for Blackrock College in Dublin and maintaining his consistency for Ireland. However, his chances of being part of an Irish Grand Slam team in 1972 were wrecked when Wales and Scotland refused to travel to Dublin because of the tense political situation, leaving Ireland stranded on two wins with two matches not played. Consolation came two years later when Ireland captured the Five Nations title for the first time since 1951.

The same year saw Slattery join the Lions' party to South Africa under Willie John McBride. The Lions' uncompromising forward play contributed enormously to the team's success, nowhere more so than in the back row of Slattery, Mervyn Davies and Roger Uttley. Slattery performed to his own exacting standards in all four Tests and was only denied a match-winning try in the final drawn Test because the referee ruled that he had not grounded the ball properly.

His unbroken run of 28 Irish caps was ended in 1976 by injury but he returned to fitness the following year and showed that he had lost none of his drive by turning in some barnstorming displays, most notably against Wales in 1978 where, despite playing like a man possessed, he was unable to prevent an Irish defeat.

Between 1979 and 1981 Slattery was made captain of Ireland but Five Nations results were disappointing. However, he did lead them to a 2-0 Test series win in Australia. Relieved of the captaincy for the 1982 season, he still played a major part in Ireland's first Triple Crown since 1949 and they only missed out on a Grand Slam by losing their final game in Paris. The following year Ireland again dominated the Championship but defeat to Wales forced them to share the title with France, Slattery marking his last international, against England in Dublin, with a rare try. He played just one match in 1984 – in Paris – before bowing out at the age of 34. Nobody could dispute that he had earned the rest.

Fergus Slattery was a predatory flanker, always with a scrum-half or fly-half in his sights

GREAT RUGBY HEROES

FERGUS SLATTERY

ARTHUR SMITH

Arthur Smith was an inspirational captain for Scotland and a sad loss to rugby when he died at only 42 years of age

ARTHUR SMITH

Scotland have been well served on the wing by Smiths. In the 1920s there was Australian-born Ian Smith who scored three tries on his debut and played a major part in the 1925 Grand Slam. Then thirty years later along came Arthur Smith who not only inherited Ian's nickname of 'The Flying Scot' but also overtook his record for the number of Scottish caps won by a back.

Arthur Smith was an extraordinarily talented young man. A farmer's son from Galloway, he achieved a first-class degree in mathematics at Glasgow University, then a PhD at Cambridge and went on to lead both Scotland and the British Lions despite playing in the position generally deemed to be least suited to captaincy. He used his intelligence to maximum effect on the rugby field, preferring to outwit opponents with a subtle change of pace or direction rather than going for brute force or pure speed. A favourite ruse was to lull defenders into thinking that he was about to kick, pass or even stop before suddenly accelerating away on the outside. Once he was in the clear, he was a deadly finisher. He also had a wide variety of kicks at his disposal, having mastered both the chipped kick ahead and the cross-kick inside. In defence he was a determined tackler who, although not the toughest wing in history, was rarely out-muscled – and certainly never out-smarted.

He made his first appearance for his country in 1955 at a time when Scotland were on a horrendous losing run of seventeen matches. His inclusion immediately stopped the rot and he scored an opportunist try on his debut as the Scots recorded an emphatic 35-10 victory over Wales. National pride had been restored at last. Within a few months the new boy had been picked for the Lions' tour to South Africa but had the misfortune to break a bone in his hand in the very first match and ended up playing in just four games. Ever resourceful, he used the spare time to practise his goalkicking, thereby adding another string to his bow. On the way home he showed the tourists what they had been missing by running in a succession of tries against East Africa.

In 1957 his leadership qualities and tactical brain were recognised when he was appointed captain of Scotland and he would go on to lead his country in fifteen Tests, equalling Mark Morrison's record. In that same year he also captained the Barbarians to a remarkable 40-0 thrashing of Cardiff – their best-ever result in Wales.

Smith returned to South Africa in 1960 with Scotland in what was the first major overseas tour undertaken by a Home Union. He scored eight points but could not prevent the gallant Scots going down 18-10 in the only Test. Since he was soon due to embark on a lengthy business trip to the United States, it was assumed that he would be quitting international rugby but at the last minute he joined an Edinburgh stockbrokers firm instead and was thus able to play on for another two years. So it was that in 1962 he made his third tour of South Africa – this time as captain of the Lions. Without the brilliant threequarters of previous tours, Smith was forced to adopt a tight, containing game. The first three Tests produced one draw and two narrow defeats for the tourists and it was only when Smith was absent for the final Test that the Lions threw caution to the wind and were hammered 34-14. It is said that he was not best pleased.

Retiring from rugby at the end of that tour, Smith became a high-flier in the business world, only to be tragically struck down by cancer at the age of 42.

One writer noted recently: 'Arthur Smith's style of play seemed so natural that it represented a perfect standard. Nobody has ever worn the Number 14 jersey for Scotland since with quite the same authority.'

Arthur Smith

Born: Castle Douglas, Scotland, 1933 (d. 1975)

Country: Scotland

Position: Wing

International caps: 33

Clubs: Cambridge University, Gosforth, Ebbw Vale, Edinburgh Wanderers

Representative honours: British Lions, Barbarians

RORY UNDERWOOD

RORY UNDERWOOD

Rory Underwood

Born: Middlesbrough, England, 1963

Country: England

Position: Wing

International caps: 85

Clubs: RAF, Leicester, Bedford

Representative honours: British Lions, Barbarians

As an RAF Flight-lieutenant, Rory Underwood played rugby the way he flew fighter planes – straight, true and at supersonic speed. The sight of Underwood in full flight was the most thrilling in modern English rugby and once he got air space there was no catching him. This searing pace brought him an English record 49 Test tries and 85 caps until the latter figure was overhauled by Jason Leonard.

Born in Middlesbrough and educated at Barnard Castle School in Durham, where he was a contemporary of Rob Andrew, Underwood's starring performances for Yorkshire, the North and England 'B' led to a full call-up in 1984 when the 20-year-old took to the field against Ireland at Twickenham. He demonstrated his blinding speed by scoring a typically opportunist try in his second game, against France, but RAF commitments forced him to miss England's tour of South Africa. The Leicester flier found scoring opportunities at a premium in his early years with England and managed just two tries in his first three seasons but all that changed with the arrival of coach Geoff Cooke and in 1988 a reborn Underwood responded to the new regime with nine tries in nine games.

The following year he rattled in five tries against Fiji, thereby equalling Dan Lambert's 1907 record for England, and his form won him a place on the Lions' tour to Australia. Although his attacking chances were limited, particularly in the Tests where he was obliged to do more covering than he would have wished, he still produced four tries in eight tour games, including two spectacular solo runs against New South Wales. Nevertheless, he still had his critics who pointed to flaws in his defensive game, usually the result of momentary lapses in concentration.

Such considerations were forgotten when he ran in five tries in the 1990 season, among them an 80-metre dash in the 34-6 rout of Wales at Twickenham before following up with a hat-trick against Argentina. In 1991, having added a touch of guile to his raw pace, he helped England to a Grand Slam (others would follow in 1992 and 1995) and the final of the World Cup, picking up his fiftieth cap in the gruelling semi-final against Scotland. When Underwood was later presented with the match ball, Australia's David Campese remarked sarcastically that 'it was the only time he got the ball in the game' – a swipe at England's unadventurous and intransigent tactics. Campo would still be smirking after the final.

Just about the only player in the world who could match

Underwood for speed was younger brother Tony and in 1993 the pair of them lined up on opposite wings against Scotland, becoming the first brothers to appear together in an England Championship side since the Wheatleys in 1938. Tony went on to score thirteen tries in 27 Tests – a ratio that was almost as good as that of his famous sibling.

A second Lions' tour beckoned for Rory that year. He appeared in all three Tests in New Zealand and his try in the second Test at Wellington helped give the Lions their greatest-ever winning margin against the All Blacks, 20-7. Even in his thirties he appeared to have lost none of his zest and was looking forward to one last crack at the World Cup. The 1995 tournament promised much but after gaining revenge on Australia in the quarter-finals, England came up against Jonah Lomu in the semis. Luckily for Rory it was brother Tony who was given the thankless task of marking the All Black sensation who promptly steamrollered over anything in an England shirt to crush Anglo hopes for another four years.

Rory played on through the 1996 season, eventually retiring after a 28-15 victory over Ireland at Twickenham. The speed machine was returned to the hangar.

One of the few players who could match Rory Underwood's speed on the wing was his younger brother Tony. They became the first brothers to appear together for England in almost half a century

WAVELL WAKEFIELD

Wavell Wakefield

Born: Beckenham, England, 1898 (d. 1983)

Country: England

Position: Flanker, lock, No. 8

International caps: 31

Clubs: Cambridge University, RAF, Leicester, Harlequins

Representative honours: Barbarians

WAVELL WAKEFIELD

Quite apart from helping England to three Grand Slams in the 1920s, Wavell Wakefield changed the face of rugby. A versatile forward himself, he revolutionised the function of the pack, creating specialist roles for the individual members who, until then, had simply wandered aimlessly from one set-piece to the next.

Previously, forwards had been virtually static at set-pieces. They would turn up for scrummages and lineouts and arrange themselves in the order they had arrived. There was precious little organisation and once the set play was over, they would wait for the next one, taking care to keep out of the way while the backs got on with the game. But Wakefield allotted each forward position a special duty, not only in set plays but also in the loose. He came up with defensive systems for the forwards, including the use of a fast open-side flanker to put pressure on the opposition fly-half at set-pieces. Furthermore he encouraged the back row to attack the opposition's midfield backs in an attempt to make them run harmlessly across field instead of forward. He first put his ideas into practice when captaining the Cambridge University team in the 1922 Varsity match and was rewarded with a 21-8 victory over a shell-shocked Oxford.

By then William Wavell Wakefield – or 'Wakers' as he was known to his friends — was already an established England player. Born at Beckenham, Kent, shortly before the turn of the century, he was educated at Sedbergh in Cumbria where, in addition to captaining the school team, he also excelled at cricket and athletics. He served with the Royal Flying Corps during the First World War and later became the RAF's 440-yard champion. He won his first England rugby cap on 17 January 1920, the match ending in a disastrous 19-5 defeat to Wales at Swansea. Wakefield wasn't accustomed to failure in any walk of life and set about remedying the situation.

He did not have long to wait. The following season England carried all before them, romping to their third Grand Slam, the achievement sealed by a 10-6 win in Paris. Wakefield played in all four Championship games (as he did every year over a period of seven seasons) and, at 6ft tall and weighing fourteen stone, his stamina, strength and pace made him an awkward adversary. In 1923 England recorded another Grand Slam and, with Wakefield appointed captain, amazingly repeated the accomplishment the next year. Although back-to-back Grand Slams had been achieved twice in the past (by Wales in 1908 and 1909 and by England in 1913 and 1914), it would be another 68 years before the feat

was repeated – by Will Carling's England.

Wakefield stood down as captain in 1926, having led his country on an unprecedented thirteen occasions – a record that would not be passed until the days of Bill Beaumont. His final game was a 3-0 defeat in Paris in 1927, his total of 31 caps also creating a new England record.

Naturally the ebullient Wakefield was not one to rest on his laurels. He became a Conservative MP at the age of 37 and received a knighthood in 1944. Six years later he became President of the Rugby Football Union and in 1963 he became the First Baron Wakefield of Kendal. He died in Kendal in 1983 at the age of 85.

One of the game's great movers and shakers, Wakefield proposed in 1930 that touch-kicking should be restricted. Thirty-seven years later, the authorities adopted the Australian 'dispensation' rule whereby touch-kicking on the full outside the 22 was prohibited. On hearing of the amendment, Wakefield remarked: 'That's about the length of time it takes to get a Law changed in rugby football!'

Harlequins in 1960 with Wavell Wakefield (by now Sir Wavell) seated fourth from left in the middle row

J.P.R. WILLIAMS

GREAT RUGBY HEROES

J. P. R. WILLIAMS

J.P.R. Williams won the Junior Wimbledon tennis title at the age of seventeen and made his debut at full-back for Wales just two years later

J. P. R. The initials are as instantly recognisable in the sporting world as LBW or, perhaps in the context of those who were on the receiving end of his bone-crunching tackles, GBH. Blessed with passion, aggression and power, John Peter Rhys Williams was the number one full-back in the world who, by taking full advantage of the new 'dispensation' Law, was able to indulge in his love of open, attacking rugby. With kicking to touch no longer an easy way out, Williams seized the opportunity to run with the ball, bursting into the threequarter line like an express train to wreak havoc among the opposition defence. He played with fire, dash and flair. In short he played rugby the way it was meant to be played.

Williams' strengths were not solely confined to his attacking play. In defence he tackled like a demon, his positioning was impeccable and he was safety personified under the high ball. It has been argued that his kicking was not of the highest quality but his game – studded with enterprising counter attacks – obviated the need for the big boot.

The Bridgend-born youngster was a talented all-round sportsman and captured the Junior Wimbledon tennis title at seventeen. He won rugby caps with Wales Schoolboys before leaving Millfield to study medicine in London. In the summer of 1968 he toured Argentina with a Welsh XV and created such an impression that he was selected for his first full international the following spring, playing his part in a 17-3 victory over Scotland at Murrayfield. Being surrounded by such a wealth of talent in the Welsh line-up hastened Williams' rugby education and he was in the invidious position of finding himself part of a Triple Crown winning side in his first season of international rugby. However, he and his team-mates were quickly brought back down to earth by a two-Test whitewash in New Zealand.

The sight of his fifteen-stone frame flying into the action quickly made him a big favourite with the Welsh fans. He scored his first try in 1970 – against England – and helped Wales to a Grand Slam in 1971 despite suffering a depressed fracture of the cheekbone during the 22-6 victory over England in Cardiff. Incidentally, in eleven meetings with England, Williams always finished on the winning side – another reason why the Welsh supporters loved him.

In the wake of the Grand Slam, he returned to New Zealand with the Lions and his calm assurance under pressure combined with his buccaneering attacking instincts played a major part in the Lions' success. The icing on the cake was when he dropped a goal from 45 metres in the final Test to level the scores and give the Lions a 2-1

victory. His understudy, Bob Hiller, had earlier ribbed him that he could not be considered a complete player until he had dropped a goal in an international. How J.P.R. loved a challenge!

Williams would go on to win 55 caps with Wales and eight for the Lions, touring again with Willie John McBride's team to South Africa in 1974. In a total of eight Test appearances for the Lions, he was only once on the losing side. He helped Wales to six Triple Crowns (captaining the triumphant 1979 team) plus three Grand Slams and in 1976-77 was voted Rothmans Player of the Year.

He announced his retirement at the end of the 1979 season but was persuaded back before finally quitting in 1981 to concentrate on his medical career.

J.P.R.'s total of 54 caps at full-back is a Welsh record. So what of the other cap? On the 1978 tour to Australia, Wales were so badly hit by injuries that he was asked to play as flanker in the second Test, thus becoming one of the few players to appear as a back and a forward at Test level.

J.P.R. Williams

Born: Bridgend, Wales, 1949

Country: Wales

Position: Full-back

International caps: 55

Clubs: London Welsh, Bridgend

Representative honours: British Lions, Barbarians

JEFF WILSON

An athlete, basketball player and cricketer, Jeff Wilson chose rugby as his first love, but returned to cricket when he retired from international rugby

Jeff Wilson

Born: Invercargill, New Zealand, 1973

Country: New Zealand

Position: Wing, full-back

International caps: 60

Clubs: Harbour

Representative honours: Otago

JEFF WILSON

J eff Wilson's versatility is almost frightening. He has proved himself equally adept at playing either on the wing or at full-back at the highest level of world rugby, and has also represented his country at cricket, making him that rarest of New Zealand creatures, a double All Black.

Nobody can say they weren't warned about Wilson's prodigious talent. At school in Invercargill he once scored a staggering 66 points in one match from nine tries (then counting for four points apiece) and fifteen conversions. And that was quite apart from his achievements at athletics, in which he won South Island Secondary School titles, basketball and cricket. Unlike some other schoolboy prodigies, Wilson quickly adapted to higher-grade competition, making his representative rugby debut while still at school. A year later, having moved to Dunedin to become a trainee teacher, he established himself in the Otago side, which at that time boasted one of the best provincial back lines. Among his team-mates there were future All Blacks Marc Ellis, John Timu, Stephen Bachop and Stu Forster but even in that star-studded line-up Wilson still managed to sparkle and came to the national selectors' notice by scoring a magnificent solo try for Otago against Auckland. Largely on the strength of that effort, Wilson was given the nod over John Kirwan as first-choice right-wing for the 1993 All Blacks' tour of Scotland and England.

But first there was the small matter of an international cricket series. For earlier in 1993 the nineteen-year-old played for New Zealand in four one-day cricket internationals against Australia. A lively medium pace bowler and hard-hitting lower middle order batsman, he excelled in those contests, producing a match-winning innings in New Zealand's victory at Hamilton. A teenage dual international, he certainly merited the tag of 'Goldie', as in Golden Boy.

Wilson carried on with the oval ball where he had left off with the hard, shiny, round one. In his Test debut against Scotland he scored three tries and kicked a touchline conversion as the All Blacks romped away to a 51-15 win. But he found the going tougher against England where, despite landing three penalties, he missed a number of other kicks and the match was lost 15-9. In truth, Wilson was a reluctant goal-kicker . . . but he just happened to be the best in the All Black team at the time.

The emergence of Jonah Lomu and the return of Kirwan led to Wilson being sidelined for a season but with John Hart as the new All

Black coach, Wilson was restored to the side and between 1996 and 1999 played in 41 consecutive Tests. When Christian Cullen also came onto the scene, Hart was left with a surplus of outstanding wingers and so he decided to play Wilson at full-back from time to time. Hart was unstinting in his praise of Wilson's adaptability, labelling him the best all-round player in the world, pointing that Wilson could run, kick, defend, do just about anything on a rugby pitch. And whatever task he performed, he did it with skill, style and polish. Above all, he could score tries, running in five against Fiji in 1997 and four against Samoa two years later. But when it came to the 1999 World Cup, New Zealand were stunned 43-31 by France in the semi-finals. For New Zealand rugby it was a shattering blow.

Exhausted by the recriminations following the World Cup exit, Wilson took a break from rugby at the end of the 2000 Super 12 series but returned the following year to play six more Tests – four as a wing and two at full-back. In the process he scored five tries to bring his total to 44 in just 60 Tests, second only to Cullen in the all-time New Zealand list. Then, at 29, Mr Versatile decided to retire from rugby and resume his cricket career.

STU WILSON

S tu Wilson was always game for a laugh. However, Australians didn't see the funny side when Wilson and fellow All Black Bernie Fraser wrote a book called *Ebony and Ivory* in which they claimed that some of the New Zealand team had been deliberately poisoned prior to the third Test in the 1980 Bledisloe Cup as part of an Australian betting scam. With precious little evidence to support the conspiracy theory, it was dismissed as either a bad joke or a way of boosting book sales, but the episode left a nasty taste in Australian mouths and, following hot on the heels of a spat with David Campese, meant that whilst Wilson was revered in his homeland he was none too popular on the other side of the Tasman Sea.

Wilson was just about the perfect identikit winger. Some players in

All Blacks captain Stu Wilson (centre) arrives in the UK with the rest of the squad for the 1983 tour of England and Scotland

that position, such as Rory Underwood, relied on sheer pace; others, such as Gerald Davies, boasted fancy footwork; then there is Jonah Lomu who is a battering ram. Wilson combined all three facets of wing play. He wasn't as strong as Lomu but he was a tough competitor and that, added to his jinks, swerves and devastating acceleration, made him one of the most exciting and dangerous players of modern times.

A promising schoolboy player, Wilson began to make great strides as a wing when he packed up smoking in 1973. After gaining selection for New Zealand Colts, Wellington (for whom he scored sixteen tries in fifteen games in his first season) and North Island, he was a member of the 1976 national side that visited Argentina under the leadership of Graham Mourie. Within a year he was making his Test debut in an 18-13 defeat against France in Toulouse. He did not have to wait long for revenge, scoring a try in his second Test as the French were defeated 15-3 in Paris eight days later. He went on to score 19 tries in just 34 Tests – a New Zealand record until it was overhauled by another great winger, John Kirwan.

He marked his first meetings with Australia in 1978 by scoring tries in the second and third Tests as New Zealand won the Bledisloe Cup series 2-1 and then starred on the All Blacks' Grand Slam tour of Britain and Ireland, going over for his team's only try in the tense 13-12 victory over Wales. An injured finger put him out of the contentious 1980 Bledisloe Cup after the first Test but he bounced back from that disappointment with a brilliant solo performance against the touring Scots in 1981, crowned by a hat-trick of tries in the second Test at Auckland. South Africa provided tougher opposition but Wilson produced crucial tries in the first and third Tests to see the All Blacks home 2-1.

In 1982 he came face-to-face with a brash nineteen-year-old called David Campese who immediately succeeded in getting under Wilson's skin by saying he'd never heard of him. Vowing retribution, Wilson was left with egg on his face as, with his first touch of the ball, Campese sold him the trademark dummy that would fool many an opponent in years to come. Once again, however, Wilson showed that sign of greatness by roaring back to form with a vengeance, taking out his frustration on the 1983 British Lions. His hat-trick in the fourth Test broke Ian Kirkpatrick's Test try-scoring record.

He was chosen to lead the All Blacks on the 1983 tour of England and Scotland but it was an unhappy experience and he retired the following year to concentrate on his work as a real estate agent and TV rugby commentator. With 104 first-class tries to his name, Stu Wilson is right up there with the all-time greats. Just don't repeat it in Australia..

Stu Wilson

Born: Gore, New Zealand, 1955

Country: New Zealand

Position: Wing

International caps: 34

Clubs: Wellington COB

Representative honours: Wellington, North Island

GREAT RUGBY HEROES

STU WILSON

THE ALL BLACKS

To rugby fans in the northern hemisphere there is something magical, almost mystical, about the All Black jersey. Maybe it's the famous pre-match haka war dance. Maybe it's the uniform colour, which makes men of medium build seem large and makes big men seem like giants. Or maybe it's simply the fact that so many great players have worn that jersey – from Colin Meads to Jonah Lomu, Don Clarke to Zinzan Brooke, George Nepia to Graham Mourie. Whatever the reason, a match against the mighty All Blacks is always something out of the ordinary, something to treasure.

All Black strength is traditionally built on uncompromising forward play but without sacrificing the flair of the back division. Whilst their philosophy that winning is everything makes them perfectly prepared to grind out results, they would rather do so by playing entertaining rugby. Their conveyor belt of talent has consistently produced players capable of fulfilling that criterion.

Rugby was introduced to New Zealand in 1870 by Charles John Monro, son of the Speaker of the country's House of Representatives. Young Monro had been sent to London for his education and while at Christ's College in Finchley he had learned to play the game. Returning to his native Nelson, he persuaded the boys of his old school, Nelson College, to play the local football club under rugby rules. Later that year he arranged a contest between Nelson and Wellington and by 1875 the game had become established throughout the colony.

In 1882 a New South Wales side toured both islands, the visit being reciprocated two years later by a New Zealand team wearing blue jerseys with a gold fern. Then in 1888 came a pioneering tour of Britain by a New Zealand Native team. Among the tourists was Tom Ellison and it was he